With all good wishes

R Bentley N...

"Now Then"

by

BENTLEY NELSTROP

British Library Cataloguing in Publication Data

ISBN 1 901470 23 7

Published by Taverner Publications and printed by Postprint
Snetterton Business Park, Snetterton, Norfolk NR16 2JZ

R. Bentley Nelstrop – The Author

A dirty boot yeoman farmer – lucky enough to have brilliant parents and a good education to the age of 16, when he quickly left school to farm with an aged and lame father.

Lucky to get the Tenancy of Westfield Farm as third generation tenant aged 21 and to marry a wonderful wife four years later.

Privileged to work with great farm workers, neighbours, advisors and professionals and then having produced four sons to have a period of enjoying their childhood, adulthood and more recently their marriage to lovely girls and the super grandchildren.

Witnessed a very exciting agricultural revolution, crops, varieties, machinery, science and application.

Found time to do my bit on various committees, including churchwarden, various NFU Committees, the Regional Panel and becoming Chairman of both Council of NIAB and Chairman of NIAB Trustees. Also to do a little consultancy work, especially when the sons needed a bit of space and responsibility.

A lot of luck with timing, life decisions and land purchase (with money I really didn't have!) and setting up four sons in a business of their choice. Lucky also to have joined with eight good friends and neighbours to form various farming co-operatives – leading to the very successful Branston Potatoes Company.

Good luck is mostly what happens when preparation meets opportunity, but I have had lots of the other sort as well.

I have been thinking for some time it was time to put it all in a book.

My special thanks to Caroline Neilson who is the only person who can read my writing and who typed up my handwritten scribble.

Also to Clifford Knowles, whom I dragged round, taking many of the photos.

PREAMBLE

Why "Now Then"?

This title seems to cover everything interesting and worthwhile during my life from 'then' to 'now', but mainly it is a wonderful greeting which, dependent on emphasis, can say so many things.

"Nah then MAATE" is a standard Lincolnshire greeting usually followed by OW Aya! The discerning reader may not use such dialect but 'now then' can mean so many things – such as hello, welcome, well done or stop it, you're out of order, think it out again, etc, etc. It all depends on emphasis and tone of each of the two words. It is not in the dictionary but well understood by most yellow bellies and proud occupants of Lincolnshire.

I realise that the contents of this book are 99.9% 'then' and 0.1% 'now'. 'Now' changes every day, whereas 'then' is permanent.

The memories and facts of 'then' become forgotten very quickly. I hope these memories will bring part of 'then' back to life for family and readers.

Every thing that happens in this life happens 'now' and in a split second becomes history = 'then'. All events therefore come under the heading of 'then'. The memory of all the wonderful and exciting 'nows' and 'thens' could fill a book!

A close relation to "Now then" is "Right then". It is a great self-starter. I find a few "Right thens" can turn a period of inertia and idleness into action and enthusiasm.

This book is part history, part biography and part people, who have enriched our lives and made their mark, but mainly funny and interesting things and people remembered from way back by a dirty-booted yeoman farmer.

I dedicate this book to my father, Leethem, a wonderful man, father and a great friend. Also to my dear wife of 50 years, Margaret, and our sons and grandchildren, who are the Now and the Future.

Me, Me, Me

I just want to apologise for the excessive use of the words I and Me. The book covers a family, a farm, people and events over an exciting period of history which I am pleased to have been there for 75 of them. What a privilege to be a happily married country man, with a great family in Lincolnshire, England.

What is a farmer? A good farmer is outstanding in his field!

I have met crafty old men who have survived on their wits and their ability to use wire, string and a big hammer, usually accompanied by adjectives and blasphemy, but recently my admiration for certain people, their farming systems and husbandry has changed.

I have gone off the big boys, the corporate organisation and the huge number of owners who are only farming by the use of contractors – running a business with no feel for the land and rural matters. I also watch very carefully, but subconsciously dislike and distrust the increasing number who come into farming and land ownership because the law and fiscal tax rules persuade them that land ownership is a wonderful investment (they are not making any more) and that it is necessary to farm it to take all the advantages. Somehow if I was a politician I would want to separate the long term hands-on farmer from the system manipulators. I am probably both!

I increasingly watch and admire the family businesses who work hard, do the job very well, involve the next generation early and are self-contained – no contractors for them. I also believe that a farm is a better place with livestock but increasingly in the Eastern Counties this is impossible.

I also have a 'thing' about the current vogue for conservation – I am much in favour of most but some of the conditions for grant payment are not my idea of conservation. I have done quite a bit of environmental work, sometimes with grants, usually without. I have planted hedges and a lot of trees, dug ponds and tried to produce habitats in wet awkward corners, but I am unhappy with many things, starting with Set Aside when the nation wasted a chance to establish clover leys to build up fertility for a future national emergency through to arable farms with uncut 20 ft high hedges full of briars and rubbish.

On this small island of ours with 60 million people and growing, we have to decide whether we want our land to produce food, energy, wildlife or space for the people to enjoy. It is a very fine balance. As a yeoman farmer, I favour the immaculate family farm producing high quality food to specialised markets **and** having time to play their part in the fabric of the countryside and village life. Absentee landlords and farmers are not much good at organising a garden fete and mowing the churchyard.

Ownership and Occupation of Land

Whilst I have farmed, the ownership of land has changed very little, but who farms it has. There are many reasons but mainly size and fiscal tax and inheritance reasons. When I started, all farmers farmed their land 'hands-on', most with livestock and arable, using their own equipment to do every job with several employees. Now two men on 1,000 acres with big kit is the order of the day. My two farming sons have their own labour force and are self-contained, except for sugar beet harvest now done by a specialist contractor. In my view they, like their dad, are proper yeomen farmers.

1881 TO 1936 – THE FIRST GENERATION

A brief history of Westfield Farm, Branston

This chapter covers the period of history from 1881 to the date when Mother married Father in 1936, with a few notes prior to that date when the Nelstrops came to Westfield House, Heath Farm, Branston – later called Westfield Farm.

Robert, in approximately 1884.

My grandfather, Robert Nelstrop, aged 28 came to Westfield as a bachelor in the autumn of 1881. He had been a tenant farmer at High Ackworth in Yorkshire and his farm had been repossessed for a coalmine. All that remains of it are slag heaps, which have been graded, sown and planted. There are memorials to the early family in the churchyard at High Ackworth.

Robert's brother William went to Stockport in Lancashire to found William Nelstrop & Son, Flour Millers. They are still there and the business is run by the fourth generation.

The Nelstrop Mill in Stockport (the oldest family milling business in Britain).

BRANSTON HEATH FARM IN 1952

35 acres, rent payable £875

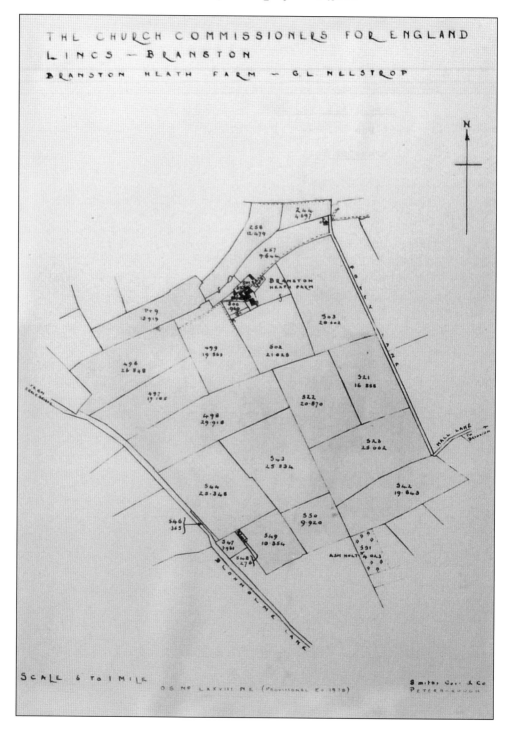

THE FIRST SCHEDULE HEREINBEFORE REFERRED TO

(See Clause 2.)

No. on Ordnance Map Sheet 1938 Edition.	Description.	Permanent Grass. Acres	Arable. Acres	Miscellaneous Total Acres Acres
	Bracebridge Parish			
Pt. 9	Part Pond Close	13.919		
	Branston Parish			
244	Betty Codd's	4.697		
257	Stackyard Close & Pair of Cottages		9.544	
258	Bottom's Close	12.479		
496	Fox Cover Close		26.848	
497	Top Nineteen Acres		19.185	
498	Long Close		29.918	
499	Nineteen Acres		19.563	
500	Paddock	.969		
501	Farmhouse, Buildings, garden, foreman's house etc.			3.276
502	Horne Close		21.025	
503	Twenty Eight Acres		28.602	
521	Second Folley		16.888	
522	First Folley		20.870	
523	Bottom Twenty Six Acres		25.662	
542	Ash Holt Close		19.843	
543	Middle Twenty Six Acres		25.834	
544	Top Twenty Six Acres		25.348	
546	Garden			.365
547	Paddock		1.961	
548	Potash Cottages			.276
549)	Ten Acres) no dividing		(10.354	
550)	Nine Acres) Hedge		(9.920	
551	Ash Holt			4.023
		32.064	311.365	7.940

The following was ploughed out under W.A.E.C.order

Branston Parish   O.S.244   4.697 acres under order dated 7/3/44.

The gravestone of Fowler Cartwright.

The 350 acre farm has been owned by the Church Commissioners during the whole of this period, and the family have always had a very good relationship with the landlord.

The previous tenant to Grandfather was Fowler Cartwright. William and Jo's farm at Abbey Farm, Kirkstead contains the wonderful Saxon church of St Leonards – just outside the boundaries of Kirkstead Abbey, which is why it survived the Dissolution of the Monasteries. In 2006, at the christening of Harry, I was wandering in the churchyard whilst all the photos were taken, when I suddenly came across a gravestone to Fowler Cartwright, died aged 47 at Heath Farm, Branston, June 1881. The death of this young man was the opportunity for my grandfather to rent one of the best farms in the area.

Prior to Fowler Cartwright was Robert Giles (we have a small wood called Giles' Gorse) who had a brother farming next door at Canwick Manor Farm (previously called St Kathryn's Grange). Both houses were installed with a beer pump to pull beer from the cellars. The pump at Canwick survives!

Previous to this was Ian Franklin, who erected the wagon shed in 1841. I think it was he who sold the farm to the Church Commissioners for England, who have owned the farm since, together with several others in the area and surrounding Lincoln.

Robert married a local girl, Fanny Bateman of Snelland, a small village near Wragby and they happily produced a large family very quickly. Gertrude (Auntie Gertie) was born in 1884 and the first seven children were at an average spacing of 13 months with numbers three, four and five all having their birthdays in succeeding Marches.

Number 6 child, a boy, died in infancy and my father, George Leethem, was the seventh child with five older sisters. Grandmother advertised in the *Lincolnshire Echo* for a Governess for five little girls – oldest six! The breakfast room adjacent the kitchen was taken over as the school room presided over by Miss Howard who I met many years later.

Robert and Fanny went on to produce three more children – two girls and the tenth a boy – Uncle Frank, whose successors now farm very successfully at Leadenham.

I can just remember all seven aunts, six of whom were spinsters and who died in reverse order – youngest first with Aunt Gertie dying in 1977 aged 92.

The favourite photo of Robert and Fanny with their nine children at Westfield. All the girls dresses are homemade. The two eldest in blue, the other five in green. The three girls in the back row all had their birthdays in succeeding Marchs.

Life was hard through the late 1890s and up to the outbreak of the first war. Life was about hard work, no spending, church twice on Sunday, and self sufficiency with food being home grown, all clothes made, and Grandmother having a weekly stall on the butter market at Lincoln to sell poultry, eggs, butter, cream, cheese, vegetables, flowers, berries, holly etc.

Grandfather, for a period from 1885 to 1891 approx., was surveyor for the parish highways, including Heighington, Nocton and Potterhanworth. I have his book for 1885/86 with names, payment, materials and stores accounts. Most labourer's signatures for wages of approx 10/-. to 6/8d (50-34p) are an X.

Later when the First World War was declared it was Robert's job to requisition good and quiet cart horses to go to France to pull gun carriages, supply wagons, etc. He and Walter Hayward from Navenby had to visit all the local farms to meet the farmers and waggoners to select suitable animals and not necessarily to take the waggoners advice! The book *Warhorse* by Michael Morpurgo and the show in London brought it all home what the horses did.

At the outbreak of the Great War in 1914, Gertrude and Kate were engaged to men who were killed in the war and the others, who were younger, lived in

Robert with cob and trap in front of back kitchen and haystack 1910 – we still have the trap.

an age which was short of men and they became housekeepers, companions, etc. All very sad, and having had a surplus of maiden aunts in my childhood, I realised in later life what they had all missed in their lives.

Annie, the second daughter, married Ted Howard from Little Morton, at Babworth near Retford. Their sons Bob and Harry's children and grandchildren now farm a large area of Nottinghamshire very successfully.

My father, George Leethem Nelstrop, was born in 1893 at Westfield. He was the seventh child and the first surviving son. He was brought up at Westfield and attended school at Branston and later Lincoln – going to school by pony and trap daily to the bottom of Cross O'cliff Hill and then by horse-drawn tram.

He was a good sportsman, playing football and cricket and was also a boxer and played tennis until his lameness stopped him.

My father was 22 at the outbreak of the Great War and immediately volunteered and joined the Lincolnshire Yeomanry, being away for five Christmases from 1914-18 – more about his war later. He returned home to farm and there is a gap of 18 years between 1918 and marrying my mother in 1936 where I know nothing! – no photos, no

Grandparents returning from church in the trap.

Robert and Fanny at Westfield with children and grandchildren – probably their Golden Wedding, 1933.

records. As far as I know it was a life of farming, markets, tennis and running after his sisters and elderly parents. It was also a time of the Great Depression, when the Nelstrops were one of the few families in the locality to survive.

Modern facilities of electricity, mains water and telephone were not introduced until much later. The phone in 1932, electricity and water around 1955. Light was supplied by oil lamp and candles, cooking by black-lead grates, and water for drinking was pumped from the well outside the back door. Soft water for washing came from the cistern which collected all the house roof water. 280 strokes of the hand pump filled the tank in the roof and this had to be done three or four times a week.

The room in the house which is now the cloakroom was the dairy, with its pansions, racks and separator in the centre. Here cream and butter were produced for consumption and sale.

The farm buildings – several of which have survived – were designed for over-wintered cattle, milling and mixing home produced feeds, carpenter's shop, hay storage, stables for cart horses together with chaff house, root house, bull boxes, etc.

For many years cattle were summered on Trentside grassland or the marshes near the east coast and wintered at home to produce manure and utilise the straw. They would be driven and not taken by lorry!

On a Friday in September 1911 a disastrous fire took place. Threshing was taking place in the yard after harvest and before the casual Irish workers went back to Ireland, when a spark from the steam engine set the stack on fire. Unfortunately the threshed straw had been carted directly to the crew yards in preparation for the stock coming in, so the fire spread rapidly burning the other stacks, all the crew yard buildings and was heading for the farmhouse. My grandparents were at the market and when the fire brigade (and many friends and neighbours who heard about the fire at market) arrived the fire was well advanced. They soon pumped the pond dry and all available hands set to to evacuate Westfield House, taking all contents down the garden. The Irish casuals first had to rescue their beer from the cellar and take it to safety to the wood (approximately three-quarters of a mile) before returning to help fight the fire!

Fortunately the wind changed and the danger passed. The stone walls affected by the fire are red and it can still be seen exactly where the fire got to.

This destruction of all the winter feed and bedding was very serious and the good neighbours all did their bit including Harry Neesham from next door Lodge Farm, Canwick, who sent two dray loads of straw next morning. The two families are still neighbours and the grandchildren and great grandchildren are good friends and good neighbours 103 years later.

The fire, September 1911 – Alice's letter to Gertie

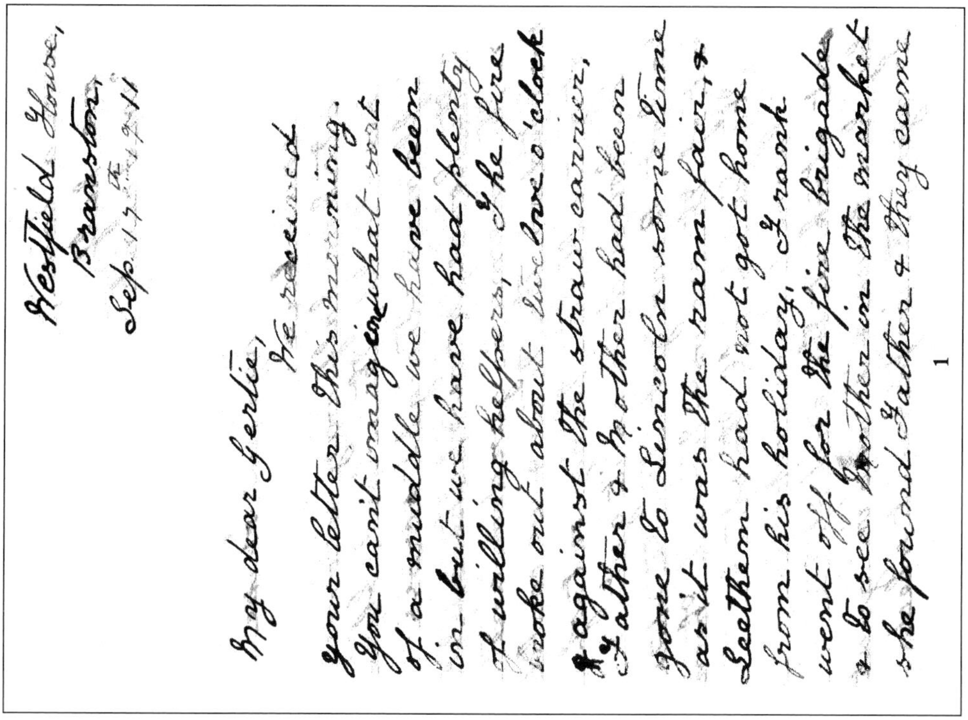

Westfield House,
Bramston,
Sep. 17th Sept 1911

My dear Gertie,

We received your letter this morning. You can't imagine what sort of a muddle we have been in but we have had plenty of willing helpers. The fire broke out about five hrs o'clock against the straw carrier, & Father & Mother had been gone to Lowestoft some time as it was the room fair, & Leethem had not got home from his holiday, Frank went off for the fire brigade & to see Brother on the market & she formed Father & they came

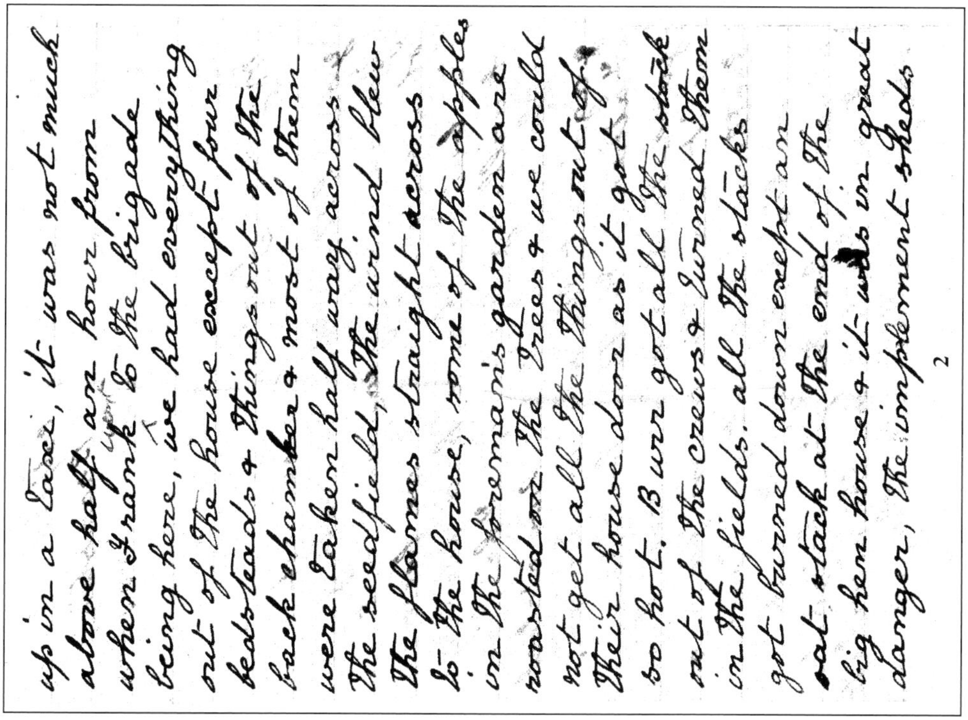

up in a tract, it was not much above half an hour from when Frank got to the brigade being here, we had everything out of the house except four bedsteads & things out of the back chamber & most of them were taken half way across the readfield, the wood blew the flames straight across to the house, some of the apples in the fireman's garden are roasted on the trees & we could not get all the things out of their house door as it got so hot. B we got all the stock out of the crews & turned them on the fields. all the stacks got burned down except an oat stack at the end of the big hen house & it was in great danger, the implement sheds

at the end of the yard got burnt
down & all the things on them.
The crew is burnt down against
the root-house, & the manure is
burnt in all the crews & the
lumbrils charred, all the cow-
crew was on fire on the floor
when the brigade got here: but
they got the hose on directly &
played on it, if they had been
ten minutes later I don't
think the house would possibly
have been saved as all the
wooden sheds would have
been on fire, I should think
we had over a hundred helpers
by xo by xo & after simply galloped
their pony from Linston when
they heard about it & were
real good helpers, their pony
had to go in the fowl places
across the paddock, father

3

went into the barn & found
someone had taken a burning
coat in & some hand was
smouldering but he threw them
all out & no other damage was
done in there, we have got a
few of the picture &glasses
smashed but not as many
other things as I expected, the
hall is damaged a good bit
& it has taken the shine off
the cleaning, the Irishmen
would get the beer out & spilt
some on the passage. we got
the stair carpet up before any
men came to help us, a lot of
people offered us beds but we
did not take any, except
Frank went to Mr Burns.
The brigade did not go until
12/5.m & then 2 men stayed
in the yard all night, Annie

4

fowls are roasted & one house burnt down, but no other lives lost, one of the firemen had his moustache front off & another his eyebrows & they had blisters all over their hands.

With love

A.H.

S. has seen over Chronicle

6

was here by 4.30 on Sat. morning to help us, & we had Mr & Mrs B who Mr & Corbett, Mrs Burchnall, Mary Grimes Katie & Leggie to help us yesterday, & & one going back to day & Annie can stay as long as she likes, Mary G. is coming again to-morrow Mr Corbett was a very good help he put us all the beds up & helped with a lot of heavy house furniture, he went away at dinner time, the valuers were here by 12 o'clock on Saturday. we have had every hot in the house to wash as the ashes blew all over them, Several folks have come & some are here to tea so have not time for more but will write again during the week. Several

5

My father's war 1914-18

My father, a bachelor aged 22, signed up at the outbreak of the war to join the Lincolnshire Yeomanry and he was away for five Christmases from 1914 to 1918.

There is no doubt, that having read about the slaughter of man and horse in France against the German guns, that the Lincolnshire Yeomanry were very fortunate to go to Egypt and Palestine, or I might not be here now!

My grandfather Robert, with Walter Hayward of Navenby, were ordered to procure a large quantity of cart horses from the local farms. Grandfather was a notable judge of horseflesh and had several broken colts to sell each year at the Lincoln Horse Fair held in the High Street. Apparently the first thing to do was to completely ignore the advice of the farm's head waggoner, who knew well which he wanted to keep and which could go. Other horse experts procured hunters and riding

George Leethem Nelstrop in uniform 1915.

cobs suitable for riding by the Yeomanry Officers, whilst the cart horses pulled guns, supplies, field station and ambulances, field hospitals, etc.

Father's rank on sailing was Farrier Sergeant (I think). After training of horses and men, Father left Southampton in charge of horses on an old iron steam

George Leethem Nelstrop, back row, far right.

ship hurriedly converted to taken a lot of horses and four or five Privates to feed and muck out.

Just out of Southampton the captain called his crew and Father's men and told them that during the voyage nothing would be thrown overboard. He was worried that German E boats would follow a trail of excreta, straw, etc. For the first few days this was ok, but as the iron 'rust bucket' approached the equator conditions for horse and man became horrific. The ship's crew and Father's men couldn't stand the horrific stench of dead horses, urine and excreta and ammonia – Father was okay as long as there was plenty of Colman's mustard to plaster on his food! In later years he used to have bread or toast with mustard and said he could still eat his breakfast sat on a dead horse.

My knowledge of the war in Palestine is non-existent except that Father's job was not to drive the horse in battle but it was to present the horses every day for battle, suitably fed, shoed and saddled up and in the evening to collect up his charges, to treat the wounded and repair the saddlery.

The only other story I have heard (true) concerned Father's wealthy friend, W. W. W. (Billy) Butt, who, at the outbreak of war, was a Grimsby trawler owner. His trawlers, skippers and crews were all commandeered for war duties, mine sweeping, etc and WWWB joined the Yeomanry – also as Farrier Sergeant. His money was useful in procuring a few luxuries and 'Rites of Passage'. At some point during hostilities the Yeomanry were based in Egypt at Alexandria next to the port. One evening WWWB went absent without leave and on his return was seriously 'carpeted' by the colonel-in-charge who said that he hoped his sergeant had a very good reason or he would be 'cashiered'. 'Well Sir,' replied WWWB 'Can you see those trawlers in Alexandria harbour – they are mine and I have been to visit my captains and crews.' – case dismissed!

In later years Father didn't talk about his war, except to relate the stories of the iron ship and Colman's mustard and Billy Butt's trawlers and to say that perhaps he had a lucky war!

George Leethem Nelstrop with a friend.

'Lest We Forget' 1914-18

Six of Father's sisters who remained unmarried had a very 'unlucky' war.

From an early age I was surrounded by aunts and it wasn't until I was a young man that I realised that a great number of young men of their generation went to fight for their country and never came back.

The eldest and third in line, Gertrude and Kate were engaged at the outbreak, but sadly their fiancés were killed (Gertrude's on the last few days of hostilities). The others, a bit younger, grew up and grew old in a society short of men. Annie (number two) was a housekeeper for Ted Howard, a Nottinghamshire farmer. They married quite late in life, but produced two sons, Bob and Harry, whose sons and their families now farm a large area of Nottinghamshire.

1. Gertrude — Born 1884 was a housekeeper for the Wright family at Grayingham, then came home when my grandparents needed care.
2. Annie — Born 1885.
3. Kate — Born March 1887 kept house for her chaotic cousin, Robert Green.
4. Alice — Born March 1888 was never too fit and lived with Sister Annie.
5. Elizabeth — Born March 1889 was housekeeper for a distant cousin at Harrogate.
6. Robert — Died in infancy 1890/91.
7. Leethem — Born 1892.
8. Dorothy — Born 1893 converted to Roman Catholicism and was companion to a lady in Lincoln.
9. Edith Mary — Born 1895 stayed home and worked both in the house and on the farm doing dairy and rearing chickens, etc.
10. Frank — Born 1896, who farmed at Wilsford and Leadenham, and whose descendants still farm at Leadenham.

Ten children in 13 years.

Apart from Annie – all the sisters came home to die, and died in reverse order – youngest first. Dear Auntie Gertie, a fine woman who never had an unkind word about anybody, looked after them all.

The end of an era

When dear Gertrude died in 1977 aged 92 it was necessary to clear the house and sort out the last of the business affairs and effects.

Grandfather had settled an annuity on his six unmarried daughters and they all left everything to each other.

One evening all six nephews and nieces gathered at Cousin Harry and Joy's at Gamston, near Retford. Cousin Bob the eldest set the rules – 1st round eldest first, youngest last to choose, round 2 youngest first, etc until everything was gone. He asked if before we started there was anything anybody particularly wanted – I staked my claim to a lovely set of lustres, which I remember as a very small boy admiring and wanting to play with on the mantelpiece at Westfield. I was given my request and they returned to Westfield drawing room mantelpiece.

I came home with jewellery, tea sets, silver and crockery, etc, etc. When Gertie's estate was completed there were funds for the six nephews and nieces – to receive £3,000 each.

My Spanish gun had broken, so I purchased a very nice pair of 12 bore shotguns with my inheritance, which have given me enormous pleasure and have been remarkably accurate if pointed in the right direction. I hope the aunts would have approved.

Poem

Author: Bob Leggate (Waggoner) – approx. 1930

We've heard of men who have fought and bled
Of men who still live and men who are dead
But this ain't a tale a blood curdling yarn
But just a we ditty of the men on our farm.
Now first there's Bill Frith the gathman who feeds   – *Bill Frith, Gathy at No. 2*
The pigs and the bullocks and tends to their needs.
And then comes Banty a smiling young lad   – *Frank Hanson aged 99*
Who's never been know to wear a face sad
He sees to the chickens and a general bootblack
Then comes his brother another called Jack.   – *Jack Hanson*
Now Jack has performed many a great feat
And my he takes some beating at taking up beet
In fact he is great, but wait all the same
There's another called Lilly, who's smart at the game   – *Arthur Lilly, Potash 2*
Now Lilly's a chap who puts a crack to the test
Then comes the milkmaid a charming old dame   – *Mrs Hanson, at No. 1*
I don't think there's need to mention her name
She milks the cows and is great at the job
And the next to bring in I think is Bob   – *Bob Leggate, the Author*
Now of course he's the waggoner with horses grand
He sows the corn and ploughs up the land

Then there's Dick Frith the chief engineer   *– Dick Frith, at Yard House*
Who ploughs with the Fordson a'y as straight as a spear
And if all at once it pulls up with a jerk
Dick just lights his pipe and then sets to work
Next there's Bob Green who sees to the flock   *– Bob Green, Potash 1*
Who tops off the turnips like the tick of the clock
Then his son Herbert, Ah here's a smart lad
Who shapes like a veteran with brains like his Dad
The last but no least is old Dick of all trades   *– Dick Frith Senior*
He can build you a hut, or sharpen your blades
In fact to beat him one would have to be slick
A clever old fellow bet your life is old Dick
So this is the last of our workmen kind friends
But I wish to suggest before my tale ends
That we take off our hats and give Nelstrops three cheers
And wish them all luck in the oncoming years.

This poem was written by Bob Leggate, the waggoner, pictured with a horse in Westfield yard.

The Hanson family

Mrs Hanson came to Westfield in 1916 with six children. She told my grandfather, Robert, that three were hers and the others belonged to her sister. She was employed during the Great War to milk the cows, make the butter weekly and other jobs around the yard.

Her husband George Henry, called Harry, who had been a butcher at Wrangle near Boston had gone to fight for his country and Mrs Hanson (Alice Mary) came to occupy a cottage at Westfield and be the breadwinner.

When Harry returned from the war he was never able to work seriously again having been gassed in the trenches, but it did not stop him fathering another four children. Most of the children worked at some time on the farm before moving on from the cottage with three small bedrooms, no bathroom, no electricity and bucket loo, but with a very good pigsty at the bottom of a good productive garden. Water for all needs was carted by bucket from a spring 150 yards away across a grass field. There was a wonderful black cooking range, a simmering kettle and wonderful food always on the table.

The children walked three miles to school at Branston and were always, according to my Aunt Gertie, smartly turned out, well-fed and left school at 14 to go into service or work on the land.

The two Hanson brothers who most influenced my life and taught brother James and I much about farming, the countryside and life in general were Chuck and Bob, who never married and lived together, firstly with their mother at the cottage and later, in 1959, in the first new bungalow of three at the road end at Westfield Farm.

Neither had any formal training or education and I always thought that Chuck, with a good education and a bit more ambition, could have been a brilliant manager. He had a great brain and memory and a wonderful knowledge of machinery, sheep and country matters. He knew the measurement of every hedge at Westfield Farm, giving yards needed per acre. I never saw him calibrate anything except the sprayer, and drilling was always spot on.

By the time I came home he was the unofficial foreman, as well as lorry driver and shepherd, and over the years from 1954 to his retirement in 1999, Chuck progressed to foreman and then manager of the growing business.

Chuck was the fellow who took me out to shoot my first pigeon, took me ferreting, collected me from boarding school and took me back. He also killed pigs on Saturdays for all pig keepers in the area, and had a licensed stungun, together with all the cratches, knives, etc. He decorated his own, relations and sometimes our houses, together with carpet fitting, tile laying, etc. And on Sundays and holidays went fishing, usually to Norfolk or Shropshire, where he often won competitions.

Chuck, having been a very good footballer in his younger days (Metheringham won the Village Trophy several times when he played for them), had a bit of knee trouble and some time in the 1960s had fallen off the top of the beet lorry when loading it and had damaged his hip. He did nothing about it and over the years he became very lame and immobile. It is a measure of the man and the high regard I had for him that I created a job as manager when he took over a lot of book work, ran two lorries, warehousing, potato store management, etc.

He was a great friend and help to Margaret over many years and a wonderful example to our four boys. James, myself and my four sons all learnt a lot about life, managing people, farming and county matters from this true Gentleman of Lincolnshire.

For many years Christmas was a bit special. Chuck and Bob looked after the presents for our children and always came for breakfast at 9.00 am on Christmas

The Hanson family taken at Westfield Cottage. The oldest six are pre-1914-18 war and youngest four post-war. All except the two oldest girls worked at some time on the farm. Chuck and Bob did 51 years each. Frank aged 99 is still in good order and proofread the Hanson chapter.

morning when volumes of cold meats were consumed and a series of jokes and party tricks would be performed by the boys on unsuspecting visitors.

There was no redundancy consideration for a man who had devoted his life to the family and farm. Chuck retired on his 65th birthday, June 1988, which by coincidence was the date when Princess Anne was President of the Lincs. Agricultural Society and she presented Chuck with his long service award of 51 years with three generations of the Nelstrops at Westfield Farm. His brother Bob received his award for 49 years at the same presentation – some record!

After retiring to live at Potterhanworth, Chuck continued to be involved around the farm and Tuesdays were reserved for Melton Mowbray market and marketing our sheep. Chuck would come to Westfield at about 3.00 pm with the market card, lots of bargain purchases and stories of men and market.

Bob was so different, a quiet self taught country man, who started life at Westfield as the 'chicken boy' and did nearly every job on the farm including carrying 18st bags of wheat up the granary steps all day. During my days he tended to be yard man, always busy in the drier, storing potatoes, grading potatoes, loading and unloading potatoes, rearing pheasants and a thousand other little jobs. There was no need to give Bob a job, he would find one! There was sometimes a problem giving orders because he was so busy he hadn't time to stop and stand still. I took to giving him a green memo with a list of jobs, when he used to immediately go to see Margaret in the kitchen for tea and sympathy.

Chuck Hanson getting his long service award (51 years) from Princess Anne, on the day of his 65th birthday.

Bob also retired aged 65, still fit and active, and two years later had had a busy morning gardening when after a good lunch he had a snooze and never woke up. We miss him and his cheerful whistle.

Chuck and Bob were part of our family as I am sure we were part of theirs.

The last surviving Hanson is Frank, aged 99, who always tells me he was

Bob Hanson getting his long service award (49 years) from Princess Anne at the Lincolnshire Show.

drilling beet in the Fox Covert when I was born on Good Friday 15th April 1938.

Tom Stovin on a gate.

Thomas and Clara Stovin

This book wouldn't be complete without a chapter on Tom and Clara and another chapter on his engines.

My maternal grandparents lived and farmed at Welton near Lincoln for many years. Tom was a bit accident prone, twice going into farming and contracting projects, expensive and coming out cheap!, when in financial trouble, but I only remember a very kind old couple farming a few cows and helping to run the village.

Grandfather in his day was a kingpin of Welton having been Chairman of the Parish Council for 33 years from 1919 to 1952. He was choirmaster, churchwarden and variously involved with cricket, football and bowls, while Grandmother was a very good bowls player. I played with her once – she was deadly!

They had four children – Coney was a much-decorated professional soldier, Margaret lived at home and was manageress of 'Camille' ladies' dress shop, Josephine died in the war and the youngest was my mother Bessie, who married Father when she was 24.

The house at Ryland and farm buildings are still there, with the house dated 1913 now called Kirton House, but the grassland and the yard are all houses. As a child I spent some time 'helping' Mabel Mason to milk the six cows by hand, then putting the milk over the cooler, pumping the water etc. It is now a faded memory, but I remember driving, aged 12?, Grandfather's Austin 12 car to the mill at Hackthorn to collect some feed for the cows. I had forgotten this until one day my father told me not to do it again, as the village bobby had been told and had 'leaned heavily' on Grandfather.

My other memory of Tom and Clara is their Golden Wedding party at the Black Bull pub. I was appalled when their best man on his feet proposing their health said that he had slept with my grandmother before her marriage to Grandfather – it transpired that as babies they had slept in the same cot!

I also remember returning home from Welton on a dreadful foggy night in about 1948 when in a proper 'pea souper' Mum and I had to have our heads out of the window to tell Father where he was – dreadful lights, no heater in the car, no cats eyes, no road markings, no street lights, nobody else on the road – just nil visibility.

Tom, Clara, Father and baby RBN at Sandilands.

Tom Stovin and his engines

I have tried to track down engines – I know Tom had a sale in 1920. My brother James also assures me he can remember a sale – presumably after Grandfather had died in ? 1955 – and everything being cut up for scrap!

I don't know for sure if Tom had a ploughing engine with wire harnesses, winches and cultivation, but he certainly had threshing sets and went from farm to farm.

There is a picture which shows the Army involved, baling hay to send to the British horses in France in the First War and a Sales Catalogue photo of a smartly restored 'Pride of Hull', which was overturned in the Battle of the Somme and brought back again. It was in the Cambridge sale and expected to make at least £300,000.00.

Tom Stovin's engines – baling hay to send to France to feed the horses, 1914. Note the soldiers assisting.

1936 TO 1953 – THE EARLY YEARS

Westfield

The time between the two wars were difficult for farming including the Great Depression when the ownership and occupation of most farms in the area changed with many bankruptcies and much hardship. Survival was by hard work, nil expenditure, milk production, cash sales of potatoes, eggs, poultry, etc.

Father met Mother (formerly Bessie Stovin of Welton) and they married in 1936, living at Bracebridge Heath until Grandfather's death in 1942 when the family moved to Westfield Farm. Leethem Nelstrop's involvement with the village of Branston goes back to his childhood. Grandfather was churchwarden in 1897 and Father had a long spell as churchwarden in the 1950s. He was instrumental in purchasing and erecting the first wooden church hall (bought from RAF Coleby) on the present site.

He suffered for many years from osteoarthritis and walked with a stick from my childhood. However in his own way he achieved much and is still remembered by many for his kindness and wise counsel.

During the 2nd World War, Father served on the War Agricultural Committee (The WarAgg!), charged with getting the land to produce more, to plough up the grass and to feed the people when food supplies were desperately short. Mother drove an ambulance and both were together on night patrols for several nights a week.

Westfield House.

Three generations at Westfield 1938. Robert, Leethem and the author.

Three generations at Westfield 2010. The author, George and Robert.

The agricultural revolution was starting and sugar beet was a new crop but it was labour intensive and very hard manual work.

The record of Westfield Farm for over 100 years wouldn't be complete without mentioning some of the people who have worked on the farm. I can't remember any before 1945 but the wage books include Pearsons, Friths, Greens, Hackneys, Hansons and other well-known Branston names.

When I came home to Westfield from college in 1956 there were eight men on 350 acres, including the Frith family in the yard and the Hansons in the cottage.

Things began to change with the advent of World War Two. The nation needed food, grass was ploughed up, sugar beet introduced, potatoes grown and there were great improvements in plant breeding and new varieties, better fertiliser and combine drilling was introduced, where wheat and barley were sown with balanced fertiliser placed next to the seed.

Grandfather died aged 90 on the night of the first 1000 bomber raid in 1942 and Mother, Father and I moved to Westfield Farm, whilst Grandmother and two aunts moved to our house at Bracebridge Heath. Brother James was born in 1945.

It must have been a huge culture shock to Mother (Bessie), to move mid-war to a big rambling cold house with no water and electric. Improvements to the house – Esse, sink units and all the facilities that go with electricity followed – except central heating which was to come late in 1968 and revolutionised the big house.

The Aunts at Brandon, Bracebridge Heath

Father bought Brandon on London Road in Bracebridge Heath for £1,360 when he got married in 1936. We lived there until 1943 when, on the death of Grandfather Robert, we swapped houses.

Granny, who was immobile and Aunts Gertrude and Edith Mary moved in – the garage was used for two large brooders so that Aunt Mary could rear the farm's chickens.

My father visited his sisters nearly every day and without fail the family would congregate for tea on a Friday after Lincoln market.

Uncle Frank and Aunt Ivy and family from Leadenham would call after Lincoln Market and Mother, Father and I, and for a few years Margaret, called for a splendid tea of fat bacon, pilchards, beetroot, plum bread and twists, which were made every week for the family, with splendid homemade bread. The bacon, pilchards and beetroot weren't to everybody's taste!

In the summer we usually mowed the lawn and did a bit of gardening after tea.

School & education and events – aged 3-18

I can't remember anything before I was three except that in a paddy I threw gravel at the Georgian bay window at Westfield and my father took me all the way to the bottom of the vegetable garden to smack me. There was then the clever event when Anthony Rodgers and I took Mother's clothes peg bag on our tricycles and posted a few in every letterbox on London Road, Bracebridge Heath. It wasn't such a good job knocking on doors and asking for them back.

RBN with Father at Brandon aged three – a favourite photo.

I started school, aged five, at Bracebridge Heath in Miss Brewitt's class. There was no nursery school. Charlie Froggatt was headmaster. By this time we lived at the farm, so my Aunts collected me every lunchtime and gave me my dinner.

RBN at work!

At the age of eight in 1946 I went to St Hugh's, Woodhall Spa. I remember nothing but happy times. I made a lot of friends and can still name nearly every one of the 140 pupils on the long school photo. Food after the war was a bit dodgy. There were many rumours about eating whale, horse, donkey etc. Every Thursday one of the senior boys went to the station to collect a consignment of sausages sent from Ireland by our Headmaster Mr Forbes' brother.

In the spring of 1947, the roads were all closed by flooding at the end of term, so I came home to Lincoln by train from Kirkstead junction. I vividly remember there was very little to see from the window except water, water and water with the odd set of farm buildings and trees.

When I was 12, my father got up an over-50s cricket team to play Mr John Bembridge's team at Jubilee Park, Woodhall Spa. Dad was too lame to play

1950 – Over-50s cricket match tea in front of the pavilion at Jubilee Park.

Over-50s cricket – Father's XI versus John Bembridge's XI, 1950.

St Hugh's First XI Cricket – 1951.

but he captained from the boundary. I was privileged to have a day off school to be scorer and to enjoy the delicious picnic tea, but was not invited to the posh do at night at the Petwood Hotel.

My lasting memory of that day is of Edgar Gilbert of Billinghay fielding on his shooting stick at mid on – I and the whole party suddenly heard Edgar's booming voice ring across the hallowed turf "Bem, Bem send ya sumbody ower ere – I've thotty acres to misen".

I was an enthusiastic sportsman, but not very good. I was in the house team, and sometimes the school team. I remember the under-11 football at the Dolphin School near Newark we were given the most delicious fish and chips. I never made the rugby team, but above there is a picture of me in the cricket team which my grandchildren are taken to see at St Hugh's School.

One day a few of us were taken to Martin School to do our eleven plus exam. I passed, but in the morning break I put a ball through the school classroom window. For years the pane was identifiable by being a different shade.

Very unfortunately I passed my common entrance exams. Too well!! I got an exhibition (definitely not a scholarship) to Stamford. I went to Stamford School because, being in Lincolnshire, Father negotiated with Dr Tom Golby – Director of Education – for my education to be paid for. Dad had to pay boarding only.

The only letter my father wrote to me. In 1953, I deserved this. I read it before all exams – it did a lot of good.

This clever boy with an exhibition was put into the 4A forms – my expertise was in Maths only. All my class mates had had a year in 3rd form doing 1st year Biology, Chemistry, Physics and German. I was lost and sunk without a trace. I have, for the last 60 years, blamed the management of Stamford School for not moving me down after two or three weeks. They never did and at the start of my second year, I was put down to 4B, by which time I was not trying. Mr Frere, my housemaster, wrote to Father, who wrote me the one and only letter of his life.

It was short, to the point and did a lot of good. I started working and slowly crept up the monthly order. Dear Bartle Frere, my bachelor Housemaster, was a nice man. He was 'broken down aristocracy', puffed a big old pipe and drove a magnificent vintage Rolls Royce, but as a suitable Housemaster for 13-16 year-old boys he was not appropriate. Fagging and beating by Prefect as well as Master was still just in vogue and I had my backside warmed up by Prefect, Housemaster and Headmaster in my last week of term for a prank with the Chaplain's car which went wrong. The only person who ever hurt me (he can't remember it) was Tom Curtis who now lives in the same village as me.

I can't remember my crime, but I can remember bending over a bed at the far end of the Senior Dorm (Dormitory). Tom was a very strong and fit School Prefect and he hurt! At the end of every beating it was the done thing to shake hands and say 'Thank you Sir', at which point it was all done and forgotten!

I did six O Levels, got five and failed History, and left as quickly as I could. In later years it was the ambition of each of our four sons to get more O Levels than Mother and Father put together. They all did it quite easily!

The day I left Stamford school aged 16, I did several things:

1. I vowed that any children I had would have a married housemaster.
2. I joined the Old Stamfordian Society as a paid up for life member.
3. I put down on paper (since lost) my ambitions for life:
   a) to go to farm college
   b) to farm 1,000 acres by age 40 and own it if possible
   c) to marry happily, to raise a family and keep them out of the same traps I fell in and not to send them to Stamford!
   d) to own a Bentley motor car

I have recently been thinking about my anger with Stamford. Just maybe it didn't do me any harm and possibly has been a driving force through my adult life – is it time to forgive?

By the time I left school aged 16, Father was aged 63 and very lame on one or two sticks. I should probably have gone away for a few years and worked for somebody else. (I was 59 before I actually worked for somebody else). It was the period of ending the Army Conscription but not quite and Father applied for me to stop home on the basis of his need.

After a year at home, when I passed my driving test, I went, aged 17, to Caythorpe Farm Institute for a one-year National Certificate in Agriculture (NCA). This was a wonderful year, I learned a bit about farming and a lot about life. I made some very good friends and fell in love. The pub and Young Farmers' Club were very popular – it was all before the breathalyser. Unfortunately I got banned from having a car at college. I had an A40 Austin pickup truck, which I kept on Charles Theaker's drive side at Hill Top Farm. One night I went (stone sober) down to the Caythorpe pubs to collect a truck load! Unfortunately the Principal, Joe Rowland, was just outside his house when this very noisy truck came up the hill, turning sharp left into the farm drive and I think we tipped one man out.

That was the end of my formal education but I have attended the University of Life ever since.

Caythorpe Farm Institute Rugby XV – 1956.

The house cow, butter and cream

The old dairy, which I converted to my first office and now part of the cloakroom and clothes cupboard, was a splendid room. In the middle (one step down) was a Mellotte separator surrounded by pansion racks and all the various buckets, pansions, etc. Separating was a daily job and butter making once a week. In granny's day enough cows were milked to supply her regular customers on Lincoln Butter Market on a Friday. The separated milk was fed to pigs.

We still have the churn which I remember did a good job in winter but sometimes in summer we churned and churned but the butter wouldn't come.

Wartime rations and pig killing

At a time of severe rationing, during and just after the war, farm workers got extra rations at harvest time. I can just remember helping my Auntie Gertrude split up the available extra rations with precision and fairness – tea, sugar, butter and cheese were very precious and the goods were given to all the men on Saturday morning pay day.

All men had a pigsty at their cottage – the aim was to produce a huge 30 stone pig (quite fat) which was usually killed by Chuck, who had a licence and stun gun, and butchered several days later when the serious work started. "Putting a pig away" was a great social event as well as very hard work. Nothing was wasted – hams and some other joints were laid down in salt in lead pansions and the pork pies, sausage, brawn, scraps, fries (liver, kidney, etc) were made and much given away, but the system worked well when your neighbour had his pig killed in a week or two he generously gave back to you.

D Day – troops at Westfield

A few days before the D Day invasion of France in 1944, Westfield was suddenly taken over by a Brigade/Regiment on their way from Northern country to south coast.

The officers requisitioned the front of the farmhouse and all other men and machines set up camp in the horse field, north of the pond. Father told them the bridge was very delicate, but they drove over it anyway and it collapsed. I don't think the officers and troops knew what was on or where they were going. We woke up one morning they had all gone!

Blankney – St Oswald's Church and the Hall

When I was seven, in 1945, I was at a garden party at the Grange, Metheringham, where there was a prize brass band. There was a big fire at Blankney Hall and the band couldn't play as there was too much smoke. So Mother, Father and I went to the fire and stood in the park which is now the golf course. I always understood it was caused by a WAAF from RAF Digby leaving an iron turned on. Such a pity but an investigation many years later when I used to play badminton in the remaining dining room on a Sunday afternoon showed how badly it had been built for Squire Chaplin – the beautiful façade hid some very shoddy work.

Margaret and I were married on 29th June 1963 at Blankney Church, where her father Jack was churchwarden.

We were married at St Oswald's, Blankney, on Saturday 29th June 1963 with brother James as Best Man.

We returned to Blankney on 30th June 2013 with family and friends to celebrate our Golden Wedding.

On a lovely summer's day the sun shone, the lovely bells rang for half an hour before the service. The Blankney ladies had decorated the church beautifully, the Rev'd Alan Greenhaugh, together with the organist, produced a memorable service. Our dear friend, Rt Rev'd Bob Hardy, preached the sermon and we left church to 'Here comes the Bride', 'The Lincolnshire Poacher' and 'Land of Hope and Glory'.

The grandchildren were waiting at the lychgate to throw flower petals at Nanny and we were driven off to lunch at Washingborough Hall in the Bentley with gold lamé ribbon and a chilled bottle of champagne – wonderful.

Living at the end of the runway

Westfield Farm is approx 1.25 miles from the eastern end of RAF Waddington's runway. We have lived fairly happily, if noisily, through war time bombers, the Vulcan, the AWACs and various other aircraft as well as the annual Waddington Air Show with two days of traffic and noise.

During the war the base had Stirlings, Hamdens, Wellingtons and latterly the Lancaster. I think there were a total of four crashes on the farm in the war and one since. There are a few holes in thorn hedges where the plane went through – one crashing plane picked up a new Ransome three-furrow plough and put it in the next field. The blacksmith did his best but it never ploughed quite right again. The last plane to crash was in 1950, when a Lincoln bomber (the forerunner of the Lancaster) was doing a blind landing with R.A.D.A.R. on a foggy winter evening. The aircraft should have been at 225 ft but was at 25 ft when it hit an ash tree with its left wing, which turned it about 30 degrees left. The ash tree, farmhouse and landing lights are all in a straight line. The crashing plane together with various engines and wheels took a line across the paddock, through two big chicken huts, chestnut paling fence and came to rest 60 yards to the south of the farmhouse. Before it burst into flames all six crew got out and were soon playing table tennis whilst waiting for fire engines, ambulances, etc, which long before the advent of post codes and satnav, took about an hour to arrive. A big six-wheel fire engine coming from Branston got 'far welted' over the fallen ash tree.

The remains of the ash tree are still growing happily. It undoubtedly saved Mother, Father, James and my life plus probably the six crew. We still find Perspex, alloy etc on the farm. The tree has got an RBN preservation order on it!

About 15 years ago I was in the farm yard when a man in a Jaguar drove in. He was a successful business man from Bury in Lancashire. He told me he was dying from cancer (he was a very bad colour) and that he was 'laying a few ghosts to rest from his younger years'. He believed Westfield was the place where his plane had crashed. He had told his wife and family about this over the years and he now wanted to look in daylight.

I took him to the ash tree. We walked across where the paddock and chicken huts used to be and into the field where the crashed plane skidded to a halt. I found him a bit of Perspex and alloy and he went away happy.

Our relationship with the RAF and the Waddington base has always been very good. They have a job to do and their PR with the neighbours is excellent. In the days of the Vulcan bomber the aircraft used to spend hours doing circuits and

This tree saved our lives when a Lincoln Bomber heading for the farmhouse 25ft high hit it and turned it ten degrees south, coming to rest 50 yards from the front door.

bumps. In certain atmospheric conditions a slipstream used to follow the landing aircraft about half a minute behind. Usually all we heard was a 'whoosh' and the beech trees in the orchard would sway and leaves fall off, but occasionally this slipstream would lift tiles and slates from the farmhouse and farm buildings.

On one occasion when the children were still young they had been playing in the garden but had gone in for their bath when a Vulcan slipstream lifted a considerable number of slates many of which fell to the ground and several were stuck end on in the lawn where the children had been playing.

Several years later the old pigeon cote had just been re-roofed with new pantiles and the farm employees all parked their cars in front of the pigeon cote. I was in the office one early September morning when someone came to fetch me to inspect the damage! A quantity of pantiles had lifted off the roof and crashed onto the bonnets and windscreens of three or four cars. I quickly realised it was a Vulcan and that I must claim ASAP. Technically my employees had a claim against me, I had a claim against the landlords the Church, the owner of the building, and the Church had a claim against the RAF. I telephoned RAF Waddington. We had damage and would someone come immediately. The answer was 'no' – they would send some forms which we should fill in in triplicate. I explained why this was not acceptable and got transferred to some one else more senior who also said no visit – fill in the forms. I was furious but put the phone down to think it all out.

I phoned back again and had a third go at getting someone to visit to inspect the damage – the answer was still no, so I said 'you will come' and put the phone down. We had just finished harvest and the combine was standing in the 'nine acre' near the damaged ash tree. Having disconnected the header, I instructed Chuck the Foreman to follow me in the pick up and set off with the combine. I drove it up the A15 and when midway between the two lots of traffic lights, level with the centre of the runway, I pulled it half off the road, parked it and went home to make a fourth phone call. I got hold of air traffic – yes there was a combine harvester at the end of the runway which appeared to have broken down. All flying had to be diverted elsewhere. I said I was sorry about that. It was my combine and it was stopping exactly where it was until someone had been to inspect the damage a Vulcan had caused to three or four cars.

A very helpful and apologetic Officer arrived within half an hour, inspected the damage, didn't accept liability (they never do) but authorised the repair of cars and roof – all bills to the MOD. The combine was immediately removed!

One of the best flying displays I have ever seen concerned an old V bomber – Victor or Valiant (I can't remember which) which couldn't get its landing wheels down. RAF Waddington had just developed a foam laying technique which covered the runway with foam and bubbles to kill sparks and flames, etc. Our beet lorry was parked on a hard standing next to the first landing lights, whilst three of us were harvesting sugar beet adjacent. We became aware of the aircraft doing circuits but no bumps! Ever lower and slower until finally having burnt off his fuel, the pilot brought this great metal bird in for the last time – we had stopped harvesting at the far end of the field and climbed into the trailer where we had a good view right through to the runway.

It seemed to us that the V bomber, at about a 45 degree angle to the ground, was about to 'belly' flop on top of the lorry – I have often said that if we had been on the load of beet we could have cleaned the underneath with a brush. However slowly but surely it made the foamed runway where the pilot cut the power and oh so gently dropped it on the runway – lots of fire engines and ambulances – but no crashes, no flames and apart from more foam around the beached craft no problems – very impressive.

In 2000, having lived at Westfield for 50 years, we purchased our retirement home six miles away in Coleby – at the other end of the same runway.

Mother

My mother Bessie was born 27th September 1912 in Welton. Grandfather Thomas was a farmer and engineer, owning seven traction and ploughing engine. She attended Christ's Hospital School in Lincoln and sang in the Cathedral Choir for many years.

Mother worked in a ladies' dress shop and was a keen swimmer (in the Brayford pool!) and played tennis, which is probably where she met Father.

After seven years of married life at Brandon, Bracebridge Heath, during which time she drove an ambulance for the Women's Voluntary Service (WVS) and where I was born, we all moved to Westfield. On the death of my grandfather, Robert, aged 92 on the night of the first 1000 bomber raid, the families swapped houses. Mum swapped a very nice village house for a primitive,

Mother and Father's wedding photo, 1935 at Welton.

My mother with her six grandchildren.

rambling, cold and damp farmhouse with no electricity, running water and with brick floors and black lead grate.

There was a dairy where milk was separated daily and a 'pansion rack' outside the back door for all the washed dairy equipment to dry. There was also an 'egg room' with hams hanging from the ceiling.

Over the years Mum was much involved in Branston village with the church and flower arranging, The Friendship Club and visitor to Branston Hall, which at the time was a TB hospital.

On becoming a widow at the age of 55, she moved to Branston village and threw herself into gardening, bridge and bowling. Then she discovered golf and after a few lessons I took her for a couple of rounds to get her going, then she was away! Rising to become Lady President at Blankney in her 80th year. She never asked me again after the first two occasions – she was much too good for me and I embarrassed her by whistling my way round and stopping to chat to players on the course and farm workers on the opposite side of the fence.

She became very good friends with Margaret's mother Una and they went off on several outings together. As well as Mum's excursions to Australia to see James, South Africa to visit her best friend from Welton days and the Holy Land and Lourdes as a helper on handicapped pilgrimages.

Mum started driving when tests were not necessary and drove without accident or prosecution, finally stopping driving just before her 90th birthday. Soon after which she went to live at Holmeleigh Residential Home, Navenby, for the last four years of her life.

She was always very smart and very proud of her family, including her six grandchildren, her friends and her memories of life with Father, whom she loved dearly.

Doris

When I was born, Doris Lilly came to live at Brandon. She was 15 and I am fairly certain was responsible for the greater part of my upbringing up to school age.

Doris was the only child of Arthur and Lizzie Lilly who lived in a small cottage at a long-gone yard called Potash on Westfield Farm. Her mother was a permanent invalid and I suspect life was very dull.

Doris became much involved with the Methodist Church in Lincoln and built up a circle of friends, including a gentleman friend,

Doris Lilly with James – Doris came to work for Mother aged 15. She brought me up. Sadly she was killed at a young age by a lorry.

but was cruelly killed by a large lorry at Bracebridge Heath when cycling to church.

I have a lot to be grateful to 'Dodo' for. I visit her grave to put on flowers every Christmas.

Family lavatories

From our arrival as a family at Westfield in 1943 until approximately 1960, the main toilet was not a 'wc' but a five-holer.

The owner and family went out the front door to the three-holer for two adults and one child. The domestic staff and farm staff approached the two-holer from the back of the house. Part of the reason was that until mains water arrived, flushing the one upstairs lavatory used too much precious water! I remember it as very draughty and not much fun in the winter. This double loo under one roof has now gone but the same five-holer arrangement still exists and is in workable order next door at the Manor Farm, Bracebridge Heath.

Forgotten skills

Sharpening things – Several of the farm men carried a 6" long wetstone in their waistcoat pockets (yes! most of them wore a waistcoat over their collarless shirt) whether they were hedging, scything, hoeing or using their pocket knife. The appearance of the carborundum stone, a bit of spit and two or three precise strokes would put a razor-sharp edge on the tools.

All hedges were cut with an upward stroke and on a small well-kept hedge a good man with sharp knife could do a side at walking pace. Dick Frith however used to strop his pocket knife and cut throat razor by removing his leather trouser belt and using it with a bit of spit.

The serrated knives on reapers and binders were always in need of a good sharpen. When I was a boy this was my father's job – dressed in khaki smock with the binder band belt and puffing his pipe he had a special trestle which held the knife – first a rough stone was used, then a carborundum or special 'reaper file'. Each mower and binder had at least two knives and often new sections were required before the sharpening process started.

Waggon ropes – did many important jobs and the knotting, tightening and tying was an art, which I never mastered, although I was shown dozens of times. These days loads are secured with straps and ratchets.

The operation of a **yard brush** is a skill which most people today can't do properly. A good brusher with method and knack is a joy to behold. Several of my retired farming friends are not allowed on modern machinery, but are very welcome to "drive a brush" at harvest time and when loading lorries.

Potato riddling by hand was another skill I couldn't master. Before an engine driven potato riddle – a gang of four men could do about eight tons a day, which was 160 hessian sacks weighing eight stones (56 kgs). The man with the potato fork kept two riddlers going. The riddle had a stand with a round riddle usually 1.5" squares with another 1" riddle beneath. The procedure was to shake to get rid of soil and smalls. Then by hand they would pick off substandard pig potatoes and in a deft swift movement flick the good potatoes into a trajectory where they all landed in the hessian sack held open by a metal hopper with hooks. The fourth man weighed, tied with a needle and stacked tidily. Later these sacks would be loaded on a lorry with a 'hicking stick' – a piece of wood about 30" long used by two men to deftly lift the sack onto one man's back. I mastered the hicking stick but never mastered the skill of the trajectory needed to fill the sacks.

Incidentally, in my young days, SEX was a number of hessian bags into which we put potatoes or grain!

Thatching was another skill I never learned. Arthur Lilly was the man. He built all the stacks of grain and hay, and sometimes they needed a prop. He stacked all the straw at threshing time and, apart from telling me endlessly to keep the middle high (to shed water), he kept the skills to himself.

Killing a pig and 'putting' it away. The science of killing with a knife or stun gun, bleeding, hanging up and producing gallons of boiling water from the copper – later cutting up on the cratch for the women of the house with friends and neighbours to deal with the many products of a pig.

Sowing small seeds with thumb and finger from a hopper hung round the neck – a magic sight to see an expert striding purposefully across a field with alternate left and right hand sowing on swinging ark meshed to the paced walk. Later superseded (ha ha) by the fiddle drill – a very clever machine using a violin type bow to drive a propeller under a hopper – Uncle Frank at Leadenham used to stand on his grain drill facing backwards and sow 50 or 60 acres of seeds ley per year. A bit dangerous with a set of seed harrows attached behind!

Carrying corn. Whilst potatoes were in 8st sacks, grain was put in hired sacks, oats 12st, barley 16st, wheat 18st, peas 20st. A 'winding barrow' lifted the sacks up (there are still two at Westfield). The sack balanced on the man's shoulder was then carried up a short ladder to a trailer or lorry *or* up the granary steps. I did quite a lot of this, but was never very good at the granary steps. I remember when I was a teenager and my parents were away for a day or two, I set to and built new concrete steps into the barn (still there) and fixed a new hand rail at the top in the granary to hang on to with the spare hand.

Hard manual work. Perhaps not strictly a forgotten skill, but there are few English now willing or capable of physically working land all day every day. It seems that Eastern Europeans do all the hard manual work!

1954 TO 2013 – A WONDERFUL JOURNEY

Westfield

In my first year at home, we purchased a tractor-drawn bagger, combine harvester, tractor with hydraulic loader, sugar beet harvester and two tipping tractors. The agricultural revolution was really under way.

This sudden expenditure was quickly followed by diesel tractors with self starting, headlights and tractor cabs, and investment in grain handling and storage, and forklifts. Handling funded by good demand and good prices, together with great advances in seed, fertiliser, agrochemicals and technology.

Old cattle buildings and derelict cottages were demolished, new stores for potatoes and grain and workshops built, hedges pulled out to make sensible sized fields, being replaced by much tree planting and replacement of strategic hedges. The man who planted the hedges at Westfield as a result of the Enclosures Act must have been permanently drunk – there isn't a straight hedge on the farm.

Nowadays, farming is an industry employing very few men, each driving expensive and highly complicated machinery. There is very little heavy manual work – all involved are now highly trained and competent operators. From eight men on 350 acres in 1956, there are now three men on 2,000+ acres.

The things which facilitated the great advances in mechanisation were mainly power to weight ratio – we now have 200hp tractors, a fraction of the weight of the 8hp steam engines! And hydraulics – the ability of a machine to use oil

Frank & Ivy and family at Leadenham.

pressure and rams to lift and move huge weights is much manifested in the fork lift trucks on all farms – nobody lifts anything any more if they can help it.

In the 132 years since Robert Nelstrop came to Westfield the family have prospered and expanded.

The family have a tradition of splitting the business rather than partnerships. Father's younger brother Frank moved to Wilsford on his marriage in 1932 – then to Leadenham, where his grandchildren now farm.

My brother and I split amicably in 1965 when he went to farm at Wansford near Peterborough, from where he emigrated to Australia and then back again to Roudham in Norfolk.

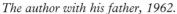

The author with his father, 1962.   *The author with father and mother.*

End of school 1954, to marriage 1963

This is quite a long period of my life and very little to write about. There are separate chapters on the 'Young Farmers' Club' and 'Girlfriends and courting', which seemed to take up most of the time when I wasn't working on the farm! Manual work was still very much the order of the day with grain in sacks, fertiliser and seed in 1 cwt bags, bales, sugar beet and potatoes still involving much hand work.

I farmed a few laying hens in batteries and fattened some pigs, which I bought in the market and sold privately to a local butcher. This earned me a bit of money to buy my first car – an Austin A30 – not very exciting and I soon graduated to a Morris 1000 – wow!

I only ever wanted to farm, so was delighted when Father took me into partnership closely followed by becoming tenant at Westfield. Father by now was very lame and aged 67, when I was 21. He was a great friend and let me do as I liked on the farm. If I was right – good. If wrong – oh dear, but I would remember for next time. I made some dreadful mistakes but somehow got away with it. He never once said "I told you so".

Father had bought Canwick Manor Farm, 190 acres, next door in 1938. He paid £5,000 for it, the snag being that the tenant Dick Pick was Mother and Father's best man and Dad wouldn't do anything to move him out.

Dick spent much of his time at the pub – his farming was poor and the rent (very low) was usually late. The week after Margaret and I got engaged, Father

Michael Scoley and Bentley Nelstrop – Christmas Dance, Branston Village Hall, 1954 – I think 24 are still alive!

took himself to see Dick and paid him £2,000 to give up his tenancy. With this £2,000 Dick bought and paid for a new bungalow on Bentley Drive at Bracebridge Heath! We began married life at Canwick Manor Farm in the bungalow.

Young Farmers' Clubs

In our day they were a wonderful organisation for country youth. Margaret and I owe a lot to the YFC – a noted marriage bureau of the countryside. We met at a YFC member's wedding and I took her out the next day.

I started as a 16 year-old at Caythorpe YFC, going by bus and cycle. Then aged about 19 was instrumental in joining with several others to form Branston YFC. We had a lot of fun with meetings, visits, socials and the Annual Rally. I remember going to a stock judging practice one evening (I had graduated to an Austin A40 pickup truck). The cattle were a bit dodgy but the instructor was very good. We were then invited to the house (a big semi-derelict hall), where we were given very weak orange squash and lettuce sandwiches – nothing else, just bread and lettuce.

Margaret in the meantime had joined Billinghay YFC and become their secretary. Billinghay won all the rallies and other competitions – notably Public Speaking, the Rally and the Quiz. The quiz team of four cousins – Roger Fletcher, Hugh Fletcher, Simon Wright and Margaret – was invincible.

The Annual Rally for many years at the Caythorpe Farm Institute was a wonderful occasion and there was much preparation at both club and individual level, and

Father and Mother with James and me, 1950.

Father with James and me, 1953...

...and again in 1960.

included stock judging with immaculate white smocks, handicrafts, cookery, tug of war, etc.

I always made a big effort for the joinery and construction competition, spending hours on it in the weeks preceding the rally. I was always up against John Lord from Hough-on-the-Hill, who usually beat me with some immaculate and craftsman like skills.

Then there was Public Speaking – a terrifying experience in 1954 for a 16 year old, but several of us remember starting, proposing or seconding the vote of thanks before graduating to speaker or chairman. I noticed early on that the judges enjoyed and rewarded a bit of humour.

Somebody (I think Lol Bembridge), with sponsorship from Dennis Brown of Brown Butlin at Ruskington, had a brilliant idea for the young farmers to have a 'decorated floats' competition annually at the Lincolnshire Show. It started approximately 1960 and is still going strong with an annual theme. I can remember having a lot of fun for two or three years before getting to the age of 25. We were definitely robbed of first prize in the year that Branston YFC did 'Polyploid and the Sugar Beats!" The judges had no sense of humour!!

Later Margaret judged the competition with Richard Grant from Langrick near Boston several years after we were married and for many years the standard of the exhibits improved, as did the capacity of hidden water tanks and pumps for the second day flour and water fight in the ring – very good fun for the YFC members and all spectators at the show.

It is sad that many clubs have disappeared and that the wonderful movement is in decline. There are so many interesting things for the youth of today to do. There are less farmers and a tendency for young people to stay at schools until 18 and then go to university.

In its heyday most of the YFC members had left school at 16 and there were no other youth activities. The social competitions and dances were great fun and all very innocent!

Courting

No names mentioned and I know I am on dangerous ground. Just a few notes and comments on innocent activity and strategy.

I am particularly delighted that I remain very good friends with several girls I took out and Margaret teases me that I have got a 'very soft spot for several ex's'.

Tennis was a great activity with lots of great fun. Tennis afternoons in our smart 'whites' was the county summer social activity.

My speciality to woo the girls was to go somewhere interesting with a picnic and a rug – I supplied the rug and the lady was invited to produce the picnic! A 'Chauvinistic Pig's' way of sorting the wheat from the chaff.

Westfield Farm, 1953 to 2013

Index

Introduction to Westfield Farm

In this part of the book I shall attempt to mark the changes which have taken place based on Westfield Farm in the last 60 years. There is no doubt that it has been the most exciting period of change in farming, including plant breeding and agrochemicals and the use of power and hydraulics and massive mechanical advances. This has meant much reduced labour so that the current farm worker is a highly skilled operator much regulated by 'Elf and Safety' and prepared to work long hours with sophisticated machinery. 60 years ago, most farms including Westfield were still 'mixed' with cattle and a house cow, breeding sheep, a few pigs, laying hens and ducks. My interest in sheep meant that they survived longer than the others, but we changed from a breeding flock to fattening bought-in lambs on arable by products.

Cropping 1953 and 2013

The chart below shows the change in cropping.

	Westfield 1953	Westfield 2013	Total (Robert Nelstrop Farms) 2013
Wheat	80	90	550
Barley	100 malting	90	550 (400 seed/150 malting)
Sugar beet	40	80	350
Potatoes	10	40	160
Vining peas	nil 50 grown 1970-1990		nil
Oilseed rape	nil	30	300
Linseed/winter beans	nil	-	100
Roots for sheep	10	-	-
Permanent grass	40	5	10
Leys for grazing/hay	60	-	-
Leys for herbage seed	nil Ryegrass and fescue 1960-1994		-
Environmental grass etc	nil	3	10
Wood and waste	10	12	70
	350 acres	350 acres	2,100 acres

Westfield Farm – the land

The soil is easy working Oolitic limestone over a good and important sticky subsoil. Grandfather knew what he was doing when he came in 1881. There is a saying that the nearer to Lincoln Cathedral the better the Lincoln Heath and the further away from the Cathedral the better the Lincolnshire Fens. There is some stone but not as much as surrounding farms. It is not a high yielding wheat farm, but with a good rotation it is productive and reliable. With irrigation installed in 1983, it will grow quality potatoes for the packing trade.

It is clear of wild oats and blackgrass, so grows mainly seed barley on contract, feed wheat (not good at milling). It is know as boy's land (sometimes girl's land) but needs farming well and kindly. Interestingly it is not suitable for the new trend of high tech combinable crops – it needs a good rotation, and enjoys regular ploughing.

Labour

	Westfield 1953 (350 acres)	2013 (2100 acres)
Full-time men	8 + boss	3 + boss
Casuals	for beet and potato picking	for wild oats/weed beet potato harvesting

Livestock

	Westfield 1953	2013
Store cattle for wintering	50	No livestock
Lambs, ewes and lambs fattened	120	

At this point I can no longer compare Westfield 1953 with 2013, so I think it is useful as an historical note to have a subchapter on houses, buildings, facilities and communications, each crop, development and changes, machinery handling and the movement to bulk.

Sheep

As most of my friends know and all my family tolerate and tease, I have always been a sheep farmer and I can't remember a time when Westfield Farm hasn't had sheep in the paddocks in the summer.

In my younger days we had the traditional flock of approx 150 Suffolk Cross ewes with a part-time shepherd, lots of hard work fencing, clagging and continual attention to the feet and footrot and 10-15 acres of kale and swedes specially grown for fattening the lambs. Chuck and I did the lambing with a shepherd's hut with a coke fire and all sheep outside in a hurdled pen in the yard, and we also did the shearing; about 40 a day with a petrol engine machine – we drank a lot of shandy!

Father and I regularly attended markets at Sleaford on a Monday and Lincoln on a Tuesday and I enjoyed the thrill of buying and selling.

This all changed in the '70s when good electric fencing became available and when we started growing vining peas and herbage seeds. Out went the ewes and we built up a fattening enterprise by annually buying up to 2700 lambs mainly in Scotland (Hawick, Newcastleton, St Boswells). These were kept in three flocks of 800-900 which came in September and October and spent their time on grass aftermath after herbage seeds, sugar beet tops and turnips sown after early vining peas.

It is also worth mentioning sheep fencing and the advent of electric fencing – first Flexinet – then three line wires. On one trip to the Borders sheep buying, I discovered two important things – I brought home a car load of flexinet from Hawick and two bottles of a new whisky called 'Famous Grouse' from Newcastleton!

The hoggets were sold mainly at Melton Mowbray by the lorry load in March and early April, when the last turnip fields would be ploughed for potatoes and herbage seed fields locked up for grass seed production.

Each flock was based on a different farm with partnership deals with neighbours.

This all came to an end in the late '90s when my sons took over the land and vining peas and herbage seeds went out of fashion. We went down to about 1000 then to 500 when my very good friend and self-employed shepherd, David Whittaker, retired. At the time of writing, the grass paddocks are let to Paul and Becky Carter, keen, young livestock producers. The end of an era!

With the purchase of a farm called Mervinslaw in the Borders of Scotland near Jedburgh in 1980, I was suddenly into sheep farming on a large scale.

Mervinslaw Farm, Jedburgh.

A nice batch of store lambs on turnips.

There had been a flock of hill sheep on the high ground and heather, but we decided on a flock of 900 Scotch mules. Blue-faced Leicester ram on a Scotch Blackie ewe crossed with a Suffolk ram. An ideal store lamb to send to Lincolnshire to fatten.

We built a shed to house 720 ewes and were quite successful and productive. There is something very special about a shed full of contented heavily pregnant ewes lying down eating when all outside is dark, cold, wet and wintery.

We had a few problems feeding silage with a disease called Lysteriosis, caused mainly by a bacteria in the soil from mole hills conserved with the grass. We changed to a very palatable barley straw full of young ryegrass, which was backloaded from Westfield in cattle wagons bringing down store lambs in November. The sheep ate what they wanted and remaining straw was pushed over the fence to bed them.

Apart from Margaret in the dipper and the sight of her being felled by 'Danny the Ram', there is not much humour in sheep farming, but we did have our moments! Perhaps the exception is the late Henry Brewis, a Northumberland farmer adept at drawing a self-satisfied dead sheep with a wonderful caption.

Moving a flock of 800 was always a challenge and big moves across highways were done very early on a Sunday morning, usually with a police presence which made the job go better. People in a comfortable car don't like either stopping for five minutes or following at 2 mph. I only twice fell out with drivers. One man following kept tight behind me and actually nudged me. Another time someone approaching quite quickly totally ignored me. I brought my stick down on his car roof. He then stopped and he was so cross I thought he was going to hit me, but I had a stick and he hadn't!

"...hurry up William – I don't think your mother can hold them much longer..."

"...we'll have t' give you the full minute Mrs N., – I think the Ministry would insist on nowt less... ?"

Two faded originals by Henry Brewis – they tell a very good story! Top: *800 sheep out Boxing Day, next Branston School.* Bottom: *Margaret in the dipper – she was 600th in for her bath.*

At the time of the Falkland Island war, RAF Nocton Hall was prepared for full scale emergency. A high speed route was organised from RAF Waddington to Nocton, which we slowed down considerably on two occasions of their practice runs. I was telephoned and asked to keep my sheep off the road – what a good job the war was quickly won.

I had a particular problem one Monday morning when foot and mouth was a problem and there was a suspected outbreak at Metheringham. I heard on the radio that all movements of livestock were banned, just as we were trying to move 800 lambs from an eaten up field to a good field of turnips next door but on a different holding. Whilst I was phoning for information and hopefully permission, which was not forthcoming, the hungry sheep got out and when I went back they were very happy in their new field – there was no way they were going back. Two other lots were at a standstill for several days, but at least they had something to eat and we had to cart out volumes of hay, sugar beet, etc to hold them.

Later when the regulations eased, there was a problem of marketing within the rules – the markets were closed. We needed to sell and the supermarkets needed meat on their shelves. On two separate weeks we got a licence to send 500 fit lambs to Woodhead Brothers for Morrisons. Mr Woodhead was brother in law to Ken Morrison. This was complicated by other regulations, so the huge lorry arrived at 2.00 am. We started loading at 4.00 am, so the lambs could be slaughtered at 9.00 am prompt. There was a further complication that if the lambs were wet they were not acceptable but had to be killed anyway and put in a skip! Luckily it was dry weather.

One of my lasting memories (sadly I hadn't got a camera) occurred on Millennium morning (1st January 2000). Following a good party at Mike and Jill Scoley's, some of the party stayed at Westfield and everyone from the evening party gathered at Westfield for a splendid breakfast at 10.00 am. Richard Bevan and I went shepherding before breakfast. It was a most wonderful sunny morning and when we got to the flock at Glebe Farm Canwick, which overlooks the City of Lincoln, there was mist in the Lincoln gap. The whole city was hidden except for the castle, the Maternity Hospital and the magnificent Cathedral bathed in sunshine.

Westfield Farm – houses

A few changes had taken place just before 1953. The original five cottages had no electric, water, bathrooms, etc. three of the cottages were knocked down, two sold off and were replaced in 1959 by the three bungalows at the road end, which for many years were either rent free or 30p per week.

The old cottage in Westfield yard had great character and backed onto the crew yards. The stockman could open a door in his kitchen to see if a cow was

The pigeon cote at Westfield. A wonderful building built approx. 1740. Each of the 750 holes is built with a curved hole for privacy and has a landing platform. Aunt Gertie remembered harvesting the eggs for winter feed and protein and for sale.

calving. It had a large garden leading to 'The Pit'. A general farm dump, it was a magical place for a small boy. The area next to the cottage was dens, trees, grass areas, etc. The other two thirds of the pit was the final resting place for domestic rubbish, wire, scrap, etc. It is now filled in and planted with trees.

I made an error when building a concrete block agrochemical shed – boarded and shelved and ticking all the 'Elf & Safety' boxes over the pit – one end split away and settled!

Dick Frith the last occupier used to plough, cultivate and sow his garden on Good Friday.

The two cottages on the farm boundary were sold by the landlords for £160 each – now with electric, water, phone, etc and some improvements they are worth about £150,000 each. Highly desirable in the country.

Two more cottages were at a yard called Potash, together with a crew yard and the good stone barn, but sadly they were all knocked down. The stone built the new church hall at Branston. The site is now part of a field. They were too near RAF Waddington for improvement.

This brings me to the Westfield Farmhouse. I remember it as dark, cold, red brick floors and lots of pantries.

When Mother and Father and I moved in, in 1942/3, there was no electric, no mains water – drinking water from a well – washing water from a cistern using all the roof water. 280 pumps to fill the tank. A phone in the hall, Lincoln 1097. A black lead grate and cooker in the kitchen and the dairy off the kitchen where the separator, all the panshions and butter making equipment were all stored on stone shelves.

It was left to Margaret and I in 1970 to change things, put in central heating and a new office. Robert and Sarah had another go at modernisations in 2001. It's a great family house with lots of good memories.

Buildings

Firstly I am delighted that many of the original buildings survive at Westfield. The crew yards were demolished before they fell down and replaced by the insulated potato store and we later added the swimming pool. The 1771 wagon shed (stone IF 1771 – Ian Fowler?) was falling down and was useless for modern equipment.

There remains the main barn range recently reroofed, all the outbuildings next the farmhouse and the dove cote, a remarkable rectangular building with 750 structured nesting holes from floor to roof. Aunt Gertrude told me when I was a boy that pigeons and their eggs were farmed when she was a child c1890. This was originally used to store a binder, chicken, brooders and two Ford and David Brown tractors. The pigeon cote had a wooden lean-to housing the threshing drum shepherd's float, built together with several other sheds from a hanger Father had bought from the World War I Airfield at Bracebridge Heath. I remember the landlords wished to make it redundant/knock it down when I was a boy after the war, but Father persuaded them to make the walls safe and reroof it – it is magical.

Since 1953 several buildings have been erected – some better than others. There isn't a decent grain dryer and all buildings are too low for modern equipment.

The potato store has been a great success – the landlords, the Church Commissioners, would only build general purpose buildings, so they paid for shed, roof, outside sheeting and floor and I paid for insulation, load bearing walls with railway sleepers, air tunnel and electrics. It has recently been much upgraded as a 700 tonne box store with new insulation, refrigeration, etc.

There have been three (rather poor) attempts at a modern grain drier mostly paid for by the tenant. I started in 1956 at the time of the first combine harvester in the shed which is now workshop, with a hand dug grain and elevator pit. The elevator fed the old threshing drum which was used as a dresser and bagging outlet for mainly malting barley. The next year with a wet harvest looming we purchased a Gascoigne bed drier which slotted in behind the pit together with three 11 tonne homemade galvanised sheet bins. The next year the Dutch barn had a concrete floor lean-to added where we wheeled all the bagged grain and stacked it two and half high in neat straight countable rows.

I then made a big mistake on a very limited budget. We started again in the old Dutch barn, putting a further lean-to on with grain walls surrounding. We had a good pit (still there and still used) feeding a dresser and three tons/hour Ransome dryer, then when dry to the two lean-to's with augers, etc. We had five bins – one self-empty to the elevator pit, but the other four were a disaster, they were emptied on to the reversible top conveyor by an auger in each bin with very little headroom to change motors or get at anything when it invariably jammed.

The final rejig was a bit better and exists today. It is labour hungry and can't keep up with modern harvester. We kicked out the three ton drier and all augers, made all old bins self-emptying and erected 4 x 25t and 3 x 55t Simplex self emptying bins with a tunnel and fan for fairly speedy bin drying and 60t/hr elevators and conveyors. Lorry loading is under cover, but modern lorries are nearing a size to make this difficult.

Finally we built an open shed next to the pit for storage at harvest and general storage for the rest of the year. Robert has sorted out his grain storage and handling by installing four 600 tonne drive on floors at Canwick Manor.

Facilities and communications

Apart from electric, water and telephone, all employees and visitors need toilet and washroom facilities as well as regularly laundered overalls, good tool boxes, first aid facilities as well as training in all matters of Health and Safety and recording by modern means.

Also communications are vital – there used to be a boss or foreman in a truck – now the boss is invariably on a tractor or machine. In the days of pea growing we had CB radios – a giant leap forward, but now everyone has a mobile telephone with regular brief calls keeping the job on 'the road'. Very many arable farmers today have 1,000 acres and one man – they do most of their business from the tractor seat.

Machinery

The machinery in 1956 was fairly basic and could generally be sorted out with a big hammer or at least by the local blacksmith.

Mechanical drives were shafts on oil-filled bearings with cast iron sprockets and malleable chains, pulleys and flat belts drove machines. V belts and hydraulics were to come later. Tractors had pulleys to drive threshers, mills and elevators and very heavy static single cylinder engines drove shearing machines, elevators and small plant.

As a youth I always marvelled at the binder and the ingenuity of the man who invented the knotter. Wood was used extensively for carts, trailers, threshers, elevators and many bits of kit and all farm workshops would have a huge array of hand forks, muck forks, spades, shovels, picks, bars, tow chains, jacks and big hammers.

The advent of hydraulics changed everything. It was a long time getting to today's sophistication, but I remember the first tractor with a front loader and the first tipper trailer and the first pick up hitch on the tractor. All a bit primitive, small and not very operator friendly, but a huge improvement on manual lifting and the fast disappearing horse and cart.

And then there was the first sprayer – seriously primitive – hit and miss and at 20' wide (6 metre) with no tramlines. It was not very accurate as well as being a bit dangerous on a tractor with no cab.

We had a collection of fertiliser drills (not spreaders), the most notable being the Tullos, a 16' wide spreading box with rotating plates and flickers. This was mounted on a large 'A' shape chassis. It travelled in line and for work was rotated 90 degrees and attached to its land wheel drive with chains. It was a two man job with all low analysis fertilisers being in 1 cwt bags – either hessian or later plastic – and the man on the back kept the hopper full as well as shouting at the driver if he was missing a bit.

Maintenance on this equipment including the 'combine drill' for sowing seed grain and fertiliser down the same spout was a permanent nightmare with much painting with gear oil after a wash at the pond. No power washers in those days! And no concern about water pollution.

I wish I had a photo of all the horse drawn equipment still on the farm and in use in 1953. The potato spinner, beet drill and two-row hoe, etc, as well as a collection of wagons, carts, drays and Father's trap – a multipurpose rubber tyred farm truck tied up at the haystack for much of the day but instantly available for shepherding, moving cattle, taking out a new binder knife or canvas or another bag of seed, etc.

The advent of the Austin A40 half ton pick up in 1955 was an important change in modus operandi as well as being my first vehicle.

The horse and trap however had one huge advantage – at a gate into a field or crew yard, it moved itself through without multiple in and outs of cab and without the animals getting out!

The chapter on mechanical handling summarises the great advance in the production of wheat, barley, sugar beet and potatoes. On the face of it we made very hard work of things, but primitive equipment and plenty of labour were the only tools available.

Moving forward to 2013, we are growing about twice as much of a better product per acre and man handles nothing. But man is wonderfully productive with the right machinery and technology.

Where next in the next 50 years?

I have no crystal ball but the increasing population must be fed. I have every confidence that the current generation and future generations will embrace the challenge and increase production with the aid of plant breeders, GMO's and advances in tractors and machinery.

Tractors

In 1953 tractors (around 30-40hp) on rubber tyres pulled implements – they did not lift them. Most had a pulley for driving threshing drums, mills and static equipment. They also had a power take off (PTO) for driving the mower and binder.

They did not yet have self-starter, cabs, lighting, hydraulic connection. Front mounted loaders had just come in but with mechanical trip and a tractor which had no 'live' clutch. It was hard work, putting the tractor in and out of gear hundreds of times a day. The engines were petrol/paraffin with two tanks – start up on petrol and convert to paraffin when warmed up.

Harry Ferguson had just invented his brilliant 3-point linkage, which in its various forms is today on every tractor produced. Soon there was a hydraulic oil supply to work front loaders and to tip a trailer. Today's tractors have several outlets to drive hydraulic motors on machinery, to work braking systems, but generally to deliver more power to sophisticated equipment. The diesel engine became widespread around 1960 – the start of much more power available for little extra weight.

The early cabs were awful – they came as a bolt-on, were noisy and droughty and it wasn't before their construction as part of the basic tractor that they became good.

Today's cab has a good seat. All levers and controls to hand, air conditioning and radio. Some now have satellite positioning for accurate straight work and other modern developments

Whilst all this was happening slowly but surely, 4-wheel drive replaced 2-wheel drive and there are now several rubber-tracked machines for greater power use and less damage to the soil.

Mechanical handling – 1953

We need to go back to 1953 – Father had bought a Wolsey elevator for (a) sacks of grain on to lorry and (b) with a hopper (loaded by hand) to load the petrol seven tonne Austin lorry with sugar beet for the factory, otherwise everything was manhandled usually two or three times seed, fertiliser in hessian sacks, which inevitably went hard and had to be sifted through a screen on a wet day. Potatoes were planted, picked, pied and riddled by hand and loaded in sacks onto the lorry with a 'hicking stick'. Sugar beet was knocked, topped and heaped by the Irishmen, picked up with a beet fork onto a trailer, stacked by hand on the roadside and loaded by hand on to the lorry.

When the binder had cut a field of grain, the sheaves were collected by hand into stooks for weather protection and maturity. Then loaded by hand onto trailers and either manhandled onto the threshing drum or up an elevator to be beautifully stacked and thatched for winter.

The ensuing products from threshing were all handled by hand. The grain suitably graded and weighed and went into hired sacks either from the Railway Company or Chisholm Fox & Garner – wheat 18st, barley 16st (100kgs), oats 12st and peas 20st. A winding barrow, several of which are still around, lifted the sack to shoulder height when it was carried sometimes up very steep granary steps, sometimes to a trailer and sometime to a tidy heap in the wagon shed.

The straw was stacked to keep out the rain and later carted with horse and cart into the crew yards and sometimes the pulse (barley awn or wheat waste) was used for cattle feed and bedding. A windy day resulted in straw everywhere! Sometimes barley straw was fed through a 3-wheel cut box which chopped it for horse and cattle feed – mixed with beet pulp and molasses or just soaked.

There was another machine called a 'batter' at the end of the threshing drum. This machine made threshed sheaves of good wheat straw which were used to cover potatoes in the pie before the soil was put on. All hedges were cut by hand trimming, cleaned up and burned.

That is not the end of it, when the crew yards were empty in April/May, the muck was loaded by hand onto carts or trailers, delivered to a clover ley due to be ploughed out or a field for potatoes where a neat muck hill was created. Later when well-rotted this was loaded by hand and spread on the land by hand.

All these men were a craftsman in their own right with a definite pecking order. I remember that at 12.00 noon on a Saturday they lined up in seniority for their wages £4-14 shilling (£4.70) per week basic and some overtime in 1957.

So what happened after 1953?

In my first year home from school in 1954 aged 16, we purchased:

A Fordson Major with "Horndraulic" loader for (a) muck (b) bagged grain.

An Allis Chalmers Rotobaler, a very clever machine but an acquired art to stack tubular bales.

A GBW beet harvester which fitted round the new Fordson, very good on a good day up to two acres, but rubbish engineering.

A Martin Markham three tonne tipping trailer (soon followed by a second). They have just gone for scrap after becoming water bowser and fencing trailer.

A Massey Harris 5'6" cut trailed bagger combine harvester. I can't remember whether it was PTO driven or had its own engine. I do remember it was a bit slow. It took five days to combine 30 acres.

We then bought a Massey Harris muck spreader – less than reliable, but a giant leap forward – and also a Massey Harris 8'6" bulk combine with diesel engine.

I remember Father telling me in 1956 on my return from Caythorpe Farm Institute that he had farmed through the Depression, had educated me and never had an overdraft until NOW and didn't know his bank manager. We have had one ever since! (Both overdraft and bank manager).

Mechanical handling – now

The sheaf and bag have long gone. The farm worker seldom has to lift or carry or move any produce by hand. The biggest change has been the forklift truck. Firstly a Sanderson on the back of a tractor lifting half a tonne to today's wonderful machine with long reach, lifting 2+ tonnes and the ability to pull a loaded trailer to the field and load the drills and planters.

Seed and fertiliser is in half tonne or 1 tonne disposable bags with a tie underneath for seed bags for 'portion control'.

Sugar beet is handled with contractors harvesting large acres per day with no handling and loading 30 tonnes lorries in four minutes with the 'mouse', a great machine which collects, cleans, loads over hedges or ditches up to 60 lorry loads a day.

Potatoes are now harvested into and stored in 1 tonne boxes, stacked up to six high. They are delivered to the packer in these boxes – no bruising and beautifully kept.

Seed potatoes come from Scotland and elsewhere, split graded in 1 tonne disposable bags, which at Westfield are emptied into 1 tonne boxes (specials to avoid sprout suppressant) and stored in a specialist refrigerated store (a converted stone barn). In this state they are in very good order to be accurately mechanically planted with controlled chitted eyes.

The grain crop has been all bulk for many years. It has to be much drier now – 15% rather than 17% in the days of bags. Seed grain now comes in half tonne or 1 tonne bags.

Grain

Harvest up to 1954 was done with a binder. We had two, a British 6' cut Albion which went clockwise, and an American 7'6" cut McCormick which travelled anti-clockwise – very handy.

A selection of trailers with 'gormers' (ladders at each end) made up the leading team. We had a 'bomb truck' which Father had just bought from a Ministry surplus sale, a home made four-wheel trailer on far too narrow a wheelbase and a 'Mofrey' – this was a rubber-tyred 'Hermaphrodite' using a farm cart with extra axle and turntable and platform to make a trailer for harvest. I never understood why the front wheels had no tubes, no air and never went flat.

I remember one night, after tea, four of us went to load up the two trailers for threshing the next day. Bob loaded a huge load of the variety 'Abed' spring barley. Next morning we threshed 14.5 quarters of barley (5 quarters per ton = nearly 3 tonnes) grain and all the straw.

After the war when food and materials were short it was trendy for grain to be 'combine drilled'. The drill had a section for grain and another for granular fertiliser, which were sown together. A maintenance nightmare – 25 acres for two men was a good day having ploughed and cultivated twice.

Agrochemicals were occasionally used but in late 1950s we purchased a Ransome Mounted Sprayer and used MCPA, which was a good thistle killer. Some used DNOC, a nasty yellow material but more effective, before a new generation of weedkiller arrived.

Tramlining hadn't been invented, so the crops were full of wheelings and inaccuracies. By 1980 many farms were on 12m tramlines for spraying and fertiliser applications. This has now gone to 24m on most farms with some 36m and wider with satellite positioning allowing machines to stick to the same 'controlled' wheelings.

The first self-propelled combine had an 8'6" cut for harvesting 180 acres. Westfield's combine now has a 25' cut doing an annual 1500 acres of combining.

Another revolution has been the straw chopper on the combine. Until approx 1990 surplus straw was burned in the trail. Great for the farm and soil and weed control but dangerous, socially unacceptable and bad for farming image. The modern chopper uses a lot of power but leaves the straw chopped small and evenly spread to aid fertility and timeliness of the next crop. However, they are terrible for encouraging the slug population!

Whilst the Plant Breeders and testing by NIAB had made great strides in yield and favourable traits, final yield was also helped by fungicides against rust, mildew, rynchosporium, eyespot, etc. Also by growth regulators and insecticides. I remember in the early days that many crops used to go flat but seldom do now.

Our smart lorry – two shades of blue with Lincoln Cathedral motif.

Sugar beet

Sugar beet was hard work. The first drill at Westfield was an old four-row horse drawn cup drill (Frank Hanson now aged 99 was drilling the Fox Covert field with beet with a horse the day I was born – Good Friday 1938). This was converted firstly with a draw bar and then to three-point linkage. Until the advent of rubbed and graded seed, this was the method of drilling – many clusters produced 2/3/4 plants which had to be singled and hand weeded.

In the 1970s a Monogerm plant was discovered. There followed several years of reduced performance in the pursuit of the single germ – germination was 60% with a 20-30% drop in performance from the half way stage of polyploids.

However hand labour had almost disappeared and there has been a spectacular increase in performance.

I was privileged to sit on the NIAB Sugar Beet Committee for 30 years until 2012, during which the breeders and the industry increased sugar yield by 1.1% compound per year for 20 years from an adjusted yield of 12 tonne/acre to 32 tonnes/acre. This extra yield is from:

Increased sugar % from 16% to 18%

Root shape from large parsnip shape with fangy roots to fatter round topped mangel shape

Better machinery and less harvesting loss

'Just in time' harvesting giving a longer growing period

The seed pellet with better germination and bug control.

There were a few errors on the way to this spectacular production success. In 1988 we grew a new wonder variety called 'Sandra' whose tops and crown at harvest time were below soil level – a nightmare to harvest. There have been a few other problems. Virus Yellows caused huge losses for a few years until Dr Hull at Rothamsted discovered the cause to be a particular aphid – now easily controlled. The other serious problem was Rhizomania – now under control with new varieties. Weed control was difficult in the early days – much inter-row skerrying, two-row to four-row to six-row to 12-row with hand hoeing. The first sprays and sprayers were less than perfect. We used to spray 7" band on the row and hoe between, but recently four or five sprays, one pre-emergence and three or four after have kept the crop clean, with no hand work at all.

After the badly engineered GBW harvester we graduated to a single row trailed steered Catchpole which did two acres a day, then a single row Standen tanker, to a Solobeet, a clever self propelled machine and then followed a period of a two stage three-row machine – wonderful tops for sheep.

Chris Howard and I decided we could build a better more efficient four-row harvester with four-row beds 17" apart and 21" wheelings. Reed & Upton, veg machinery engineers from Suffolk, built three harvesters, two were round a

120hp 4wd David Brown with basher toppers and I had a two part machine with a top saver for sheep feed.

It was a very clever machine which seldom worked well and was too heavy for our David Brown tractors. Anglia Television with David Richardson came to film it on a day it went beautifully but events overtook us and we graduated to jointly owning a six-row Moreau self-propelled harvester, with three neighbours, harvesting about 700 acres.

Beet is now harvested by a wonderful six-row 18 ton tanker machine where two men can beautifully harvest 30 acres a day.

The only snag is that the tops are 'bashed' and are no good for sheep!

Of all the crops grown at Westfield sugar beet has changed the most with spectacular yield improvement and mechanisation.

Potatoes

Father hated potatoes, especially getting them planted and organising a gang of women or children to pick them. The schools used to have a week's 'potato holiday' in October. The potatoes were spun out with a spinner hand picked into 'mollies' or 'scuttles' by the pickers who each had a measured and marked 'retch' to ensure fair play.

The farm men with horse and cart would empty each 'mollie' into the cart which went to the 'pie' and tipped up its load to form a triangular pie 7' wide and about 5' high. This was covered with straw bats and later soil for frost protection.

Riddling potatoes was a winter job for all the men starting after breakfast when the cattle and sheep had been fed and watered. Very occasionally they made a lot of money and made the effort worth while.

I expanded the enterprise in approx 1960 by growing 40 acres planted with a wonderful two-row planter with a bell. Every time the bell rang you dropped a seed potato down the spout (a bit like milking a cow with your head tucked in and both hands working to the music). The mature crop was picked by four wonderful Irishmen collected daily from Lincoln. On a good day they could pick and load two acres into low sided trailers. In the absence of a smart potato store, I modified the old drill sheds, lambing pens and cart shed at the east end of the yard, bought an elevator with hopper and extension and filled the store 6' high (the shed was only 7'6" to the eaves). This was a giant leap forward for management, winter grading etc. I can only remember three problems; firstly rats in the straw walls, secondly getting a tipped trailer stuck in the beams and thirdly in a frosty time I put a polythene sheet over the strawed top – nearly a disaster, but I just found it in time before they started to rot, as the top 12" was wet through with condensation.

Hole digging at the reservoir – pure blue clay.

We didn't realise that the Lincoln Heath was capable of producing beautiful skinned ware potatoes and went off at a tangent growing the crisp variety Record on contract to Golden Wonder Crisps of Corby. Westfield store was built to house 600 tonnes of Records for Golden Wonder.

Irrigation capacity for 80 acres was installed. There is a spring which rises on Westfield (near the pond) and runs a lot of water in the winter especially when the River Trent in Derbyshire is in flood. (Don't ask how it gets under the River Witham and up the escarpment 50', but it does!) The other bit of good news was that solid blue clay was 6' down where we built the reservoir. I did all my sums on producing extra yield, which was wrong – the big difference is in skin finish and saleable weight of top price packing and baking potatoes.

With the formation of Branston Potatoes in 1968 everything changed. With our own and rented land we went up to 150 acres. We still had the Irishmen and the hand gang for a few years for difficult and stony land, whilst a succession of harvesters and stone separators have arrived at today's system.

Stone separation and windrowing is worthy of a paragraph. I think I was the first person in our area to buy one – it quickly went back and was replaced by a Reekie. Techniques have changed, but we were able to plant in a stone free seed bed and harvest quickly without bruising.

Our first potato harvester is also worthy of a mention. The British harvesters couldn't deal with our stone and spent much time broken. However the Canadian built Thomas was built like a battleship – it crushed stones and was very noisy and had a system of angled conveyors which sorted round potatoes from flat stones. It cost a fortune in spare parts mainly imported webbing and caused a lot of bruising, but until we had sorted our stone separation it got us going. The third wonder machine worthy of a mention was the Reekie combined separator and planter (ours went two years ago!). The field was ridged and the machine separated stone and clods and placed it two rows behind in planted ridges. The clever planter was then timed to drop a seed into a sectional conveyor which transported it down the side, across the bottom underneath the separator webb and dropped it at regular intervals in the new ridge being formed. Not very fast, but one man could plant about four acres and the job was complete and tidy.

The present generation of separator, planter and harvester are seriously high-tech and seriously expensive, especially the harvester which needs 200hp to drive pre-topper, fancy separator equipment, driven wheels so that in bad conditions the harvester pushes the tractor and all the other very clever engineering to ensure bruise-free potatoes.

Our first Thomas harvester cost £3,780.00.

Today's two-row harvester costs £165,000.00 – no engine, just very clever engineering.

For many years potatoes were stored in bulk in ambient stores which were automated to use cold night air. This over a period of 15-20 years has all changed. Bulk ambient stores have now been converted to refrigerated box stores and the harvester does such a good job that eight boxes are carried on flat trailers and loaded in the field cutting out bruising, handling, graders, elevators, etc. The potato is then carried to the packing station in the box. Most potato growing farms in the area built their cold stores in the 1990s and bought their boxes before me – I was busy sorting out four sons, farms and futures.

I will complete this section by a further mention of the four Irishmen – they really did work and unlike many did not get too much beer at the weekend and not turn up for work on a Monday. They were organised by Mick O'Boyle who graduated from potato picking to digging holes and laying sewers and below-ground works in Lincoln. He and his sons now build houses and live in splendid homes.

Secondly, we had Jack McAndrew, a man of few words but a great worker. I understand from Mick that he came to England annually for a holiday away from his large family and that he now farms a large farm in Southern Ireland.

Thirdly we had Paddy Creane, who I met again on a building site 20 years ago. I didn't recognise him, but he did me. "You'll be being Mr Nelstrop – you were a haard maan, you made us pick the harrowings twice". Paddy now runs JCBs, diggers and tipper lorries around Lincoln area building sites.

Lastly we had Mick's brother John who made good with earthworks and a small farm breeding pedigree sheep.

Just a note on Branston Potatoes – they started life as a Farmers' Co-operative in 1967 with two graders and sundry equipment, and following a Feasibility Study in 1968, graduated to a packing station to pack for the markets, and had a special line for several years peating the potatoes. They looked great and it hid a lot of bruising and faults! We built cold stores for boxed storage and in August 1993, were joined by new members, put in a new smart grading line for washed potatoes, shut down the Co-operative and formed the limited liability company. It was a giant leap forward. We signed up to supply Tesco and now with three sites at Branston, Abernethy near Perth and Ilminster, Somerset, Branston Ltd produce 55% of Tesco's potatoes. A great success story very ably led by Chris Howard and Graeme Beattie.

Vining peas and herbage seeds

Not in the rotation in 1953 or 2013, but in their time very important to Westfield Farm.

In 1966 the same seven members who had earlier formed B. H. Farming Co. in 1964 to buy all our requisites got together to grow vining peas. Contracts were on offer, huge grants available to Co-operatives and we had good land.

The machinery available was less than perfect. The peas were still cut into rows by a pea cutter mounted on the back of a tractor, which had all its controls and seat adjusted to go backward. The static viner was superseded by the first mobile which was pulled by a four-wheel drive tractor – self propelled came later. Because we were 30 miles from the factory we needed a pit and chiller and 1 ton tanks, so that we could deliver cleaned and chilled peas to any factory.

The business grew to the growing of 4000 acres including 700 acres broad beans, which mainly went to Italy. We struggled to find very good land, people wanted to rent us their problem fields and on our own farm we grew peas too often in the rotation and the land got pea sick. Great fun and just profitable whilst it lasted.

We grew ryegrass for seed for many years and in the days of NSA (Nitrate Sensitive Areas) at Longhills Farm we grew red fescue for seed. It didn't need much nitrogen and fitted in with all the NSA rules.

Herbage seeds and a sheep enterprise go well together

Firstly in the first autumn and then after harvest, the grass sward is available for sheep grazing. The hay is not top class but if well made is nutritious and highly suitable for spring calving cows, donkeys and elephants! There was a generous subsidy tied to production of herbage seeds, so a reasonable seed yield crop would produce a good income from grass seed + subsidy + hay + sheep grazing. In the case of Red Fescue there was also a very generous NSA acreage subsidy.

It is sad that in 2013 much of this country's requirement for green peas comes from Hungary and herbage seeds come from warmer countries with a more reliable summer, i.e. New Zealand and Canada.

Conservation and preservation

In 1953 conservation hadn't really been invented!

The 'enlightened' were doing their bit, but it was a time after the two Great Wars where the Nation was more concerned about food and its production in a changing world. Previous generations had shaped our countryside with much tree planting and all the hedges planted at the time of the enclosures. We have much to thank our ancestors for. Europe doesn't have hedges like we do.

I was originally much interested in landscaping, trees and hedges. The current vogue for wildlife including predators and vermin, endangered species, public access, etc, backed up the public opinion and considerable grant aid is all too much for me – too much so-called conservation is being done for the wrong reasons.

When I left school and college, Westfield Farm had too many useless winding hedges in the wrong place. My idea of a good hedge is one that is good enough to hold sheep – there were none! So over a few years in the 1960s I pulled a lot out, destroyed hedgerow trees and made sensible-sized fields for modern farm machinery.

We planted a new wood on the east side of Westfield House and planted strategic roadside and other trees. I did actually plant a 200 yard hedge to strengthen a particular winding bit which Eric plashed beautifully 10 years later.

Lincs. Agricultural Society 1990 Farming & Conservation Winner.

Preservation at Westfield fared little better. When the old pigeon cote was falling down in the 1950s, Father persuaded the landlords to repair and re-roof, otherwise it was a time of knocking stone and pantile down to replace with steel and asbestos modern buildings. The lovely barn range embracing barn, chaff house, cart horse stable and nag stable were in danger, but with iron straps, reroofing and change of use have thankfully survived to be both decorative and useful. The whole of the crew yards with Yorkshire boarded roofs were demolished in the 1970s together with a cottage to make room for the insulated potato store. The lovely old six-bay wagon shed which was too low for any use and was sinking gently was demolished before it fell. Last to go was the drill house block at the east end of the yard which had a slate roof. The back wall, some of it a rich red from the great fire of 1911, survives. A good sheep handling pen replaced the building whilst all this was happening modern farming dictated the need for an up to date agrochemical store with a big water tank for quick filling and a well-equipped workshop.

I became "enlightened and enthusiastic" in the 1970s and '80s and with the purchase of Longhills in 1986, became more enthusiastic and active. The Recreation field at Branston is worthy of a mention. I was asked by the Parish Council to sell them 12 acres – I said "NO. I will sell you 13 – 12 acres for games and one to plant up with a wood on the east side or it will be the coldest field in Lincolnshire." The Parish planted the wood on a Sunday morning – organised chaos with all organisations doing their bit, the Parish Council, mums and toddlers, Friendship Club, Football, Cricket, Tennis, Bowls, etc etc. It is a wonderful wood – never been vandalised. I think there are a lot of people who remember and cherish their involvement.

With hindsight I am very flattered that I was asked to be the first and founding Chairman of Lincolnshire FWAG, where from a standing start we began to educate and inspire farmers and countrymen in Lincolnshire all to do their bit. Our 'showroom' was the Conservation Area at the Lincolnshire Show, where for many years we had a major display with lots to see and learn. The Conservation Area at the Lincolnshire Show is now huge and full of interest.

The water supply

Before mains water was laid on, by Mr Hamblet of Nettleham, with iron piping around 1960, water on the Lincoln Heath was a problem. The farmhouse had soft water for washing etc supplied by a big underground tank which collected up all house rainwater. 280 pumps from the old two-handed hand pump in the back kitchen filled the tank. The problem was if the header tank was empty you couldn't get away with 50 pumps to get a quick bath – it needed the full 280 to prime the system. The garthman Bill Frith used to do it three times a week. Drinking water came from another hand pump outside the back door.

There were two sources of hot water (assuming the kitchen range was lit). The bathroom upstairs and a tap behind the kitchen range in the back kitchen – none in the kitchen or the 'still room' where the pots were washed and stored – time and motion hadn't been invented!

There was of course the copper in the back kitchen – essential for wash day, pig killing and other requirements for volumes of hot water.

The cottages variously carted water by bucket from well or a spring up to 200 yards away.

The farm yard including all the cattle yard was supplied by a Blakes Hydram – a wonderful device which by the use of pressure cylinder and rubber washers used a large volume of water to pump a small quantity to the highest point, where it flowed by gravity to all the troughs and all spare went back to the pond.

I have a memory of my father in smock and trilby with his pipe and a very sharp pocket knife spending hours in the hole in the pond field to get the ram pumping. There are several hydrams still working in the Wolds where there is a bigger water flow and steeper slopes where the surging water makes a very loud thump.

Bookkeeping and systems in 1953

At Westfield there was a wages book carefully detailing each employee's gross wage (around £4-14-0 per week) with deductions for rent 6/- per week and Lloyd George (national insurance). This book also recorded other cash out transactions.

Thereafter it was all a 'bit thin'. There was a cheque book with the counterfoil immaculately filled in, ie. person, item, quantity/price. A paying-in book similarly comprehensively completed and a large suitcase into which everything was dropped roughly in chronological order. Once a year these items, together with bank statements, were delivered to the accountant to sort it all out.

The advent of VAT changed everything. Increasingly I needed to know where we were and what cash was due when, so did cash flow budgets and evolved a good manual bookkeeping system before computers changed everything again. I was always less concerned about turnover and profit than about cash flow.

A good idea at the time

I suppose I have done more than my share of stupid things in the pursuit of progress and profit. I have had a go at several crops and projects which have not exactly been a great success.

Courgettes are interesting. They grow at an alarming rate, need to be harvested twice a day or you are harvesting marrows. We grew them in a very wet year.

They were dirty but couldn't be washed and dried, they had to be wiped with a 'dishcloth'. Can you imagine a row of chatty ladies in a shed giving them a good wipe and polish. Our loss (considerable) was in direct proportion to the size of the crop. If we had had a smaller crop we would have lost less money – modern methods are better!

Brussels Sprouts – approximately 40 years ago the sprouts industry changed for the worst. Previously all sprouts had been multipicked by hand starting at the bottom of the stalk and working up. The new idea for processing was to have a variety which all matured on the same day and could be mechanically harvested. Three problems – firstly, the machinery wasn't yet developed. We had lots of cut stalks and armies of women with knives in a shed. Secondly they tasted dreadful – very bitter – the public rightly stopped eating them. 40 years on they are now delicious. Lastly they were useless as game cover! And not much good for sheep feed either.

Dutch White Cabbage – we had a trial go at this. We grew very good cabbages for coleslaw. It needed a commitment to building, cold store, boxes, etc.

Carrots and Carrot Seed – not a great success – Westfield is not suitable for carrots.

Swedes – we also grew Swedes for the market and for late sheep feed.

Gooseberries – I have a very comprehensive file regarding variety, husbandry, economics, etc. We always had a very good crop in the garden and I had this good idea that a fruit which has a very flexible harvest date would fit in with other activities. Then a couple of ladies who had been delegated to pick garden fruit showed me their bloody hands!

Onions – there is also a file on onions, which were never grown.

Rams and Teasers – before the common practice of stimulating ewes by adding vasectomised rams (teasers) for a few weeks, I tried to achieve the same effect with proper rams. We constructed a hurdle pen in the centre of the field. We put in three rams with water and feed and observed. Within a day the rams had seriously fought and one was dead and two battered. The hurdles were removed and the ewes were mainly disinterested!

Pea Haulm Silage – events quickly overtook us with the advent of mobile pea viners. In the 1970s a very profitable green pea industry threshed them at vining sites with rows of static viners fed by hard working men. The pea site of Parker-Dean Ltd at the Old Flax factory on Metheringham Heath produced a huge quantity of threshed haulm which made the most wonderful silage for cattle feed. There were a few problems – it needed an army of lorries and a very careful team building a big heap with no walls to the silage clamp. There was also the little matter of effluent. A vile smelling, highly toxic liquid which for three or four days flooded the yard until we found an old well to pump it into (what would the Environment Agency say today?).

The clamp was in the Dutch Barn at Canwick Manor (now an insulated potato cold store). Straw was stacked on top at harvest time and both lean-to's contained 40 or 50 store cattle which I bought in Wales. Quite a good system – all under one roof, cheap feed, lots of good muck. I suspect we didn't make a huge profit but there is something special about yards of contented cattle chewing their cud. I was with the cattle and two men at 8.00 am one morning when I heard Father had died suddenly.

Pea sales by the bucket

In our vining pea growing days in the 1970s and 1980s, we decided to sell fresh peas to the public for their deep freezer. After advertising in the local press there was a frantic week. The first year we were totally overwhelmed by queues, jams of parked cars, press publicity, etc. the bucket held a stone (14lbs) but was not weighed and the boys doing the job stuffed the money in their pockets. I was in charge of money, counting and banking. After the first few days of 'pea smelling crunched up notes' we evolved a new system whereby the punter purchased raffle tickets at a horse box and exchanged them for a bucket full. I suspect weights and measures wouldn't approve. Our sales went from zero to £45,000 per annum in four years after which the novelty passed and sales went down until after a few more years we stopped. The novelty of blanching and freezing home grown produce with your newly-purchased deep freezer soon passed when the housewife realised that peas could be bought frozen for not a lot more.

The local refrigeration man loved this week – freezers blew up with all the warm additions. It was always interesting to listen to the phone calls that week from people who had got it wrong – the main problem being that they had left the peas to do next day and found they weren't very nice. Or later when they had popped them into the freezer without blanching them and 'would we have them back?'

PIGS – another good idea which didn't actually happen. In 1979 I needed to expand and did a comprehensive research project to establish a 200 sow unit at Canwick Manor. I still have the file containing plans, cash flow budgets and technical details. At the time the figures produced looked wonderful so I was much tempted, but when the 'chips were down' and a decision had to be made, I decided I didn't really like pigs and wouldn't enjoy the project. At that time it was between pigs, English land and Scottish land – Scotland won – I bought Mervinslaw in 1980.

COWS – I also remember that in 1967 our Pea Group commissioned a report by Lugg & Gould about a large commercial dairy herd at Potterhanworth crossroads to use arable by products. This was 40 years before the aborted plan to put 8,000 milk cows on Nocton Heath.

The tale of the barley straw (A parable)

One day in 1953, I was standing proud in a field of 'Abed Kenya' spring barley ready for harvest and expected to yield seven quarters to the acre (five quarters per ton = 1.4 tonnes/acre).

On a sunny day the old binder arrived. It used to be pulled by two horses but now the Fordson tractor pulls it. I am cut about 4" from the ground and bound in a tidy sheaf with binder band. three men arrive shortly afterwards and put my sheaf together with nine others into a stook – this keeps off the rain and gives the grain and weeds time to mature.

The leading gang arrive one morning with horse and bogey for horse to pull farm trailer with gormers and three men – one to load and two to pitch. Tommy the horse has done it all before and moves on command from stook to stook (this saves a man!).

In the yard, my sheaf is put in an elevator up into the roof of a large well-built stack. "Keep the middle up to keep the water out" says Arthur the stacker.

After all the harvest is led from the fields, Arthur and a mate set to with good wheat straw and a long ladder to thatch my stack – not much health and safety involved!

Sometime in the autumn or the winter, the farmer needs (a) money and/or (b) straw to bed the cattle.

So the threshing gang arrive. There is much activity and getting stuck in the muddy yard, but eventually after taking off the thatch and putting wire round to stop rats, we are ready for off and the small army of men take their place.

Three men on the stack feed the sheaves one by one to Bob on the threshing drum who cuts the straw with a well-seared knife and feeds the sheaf in sideways. These men have yorks on their trousers to stop the rats and mice running up their legs.

At this point the straw becomes forcibly detached from the grain and the pulse which through a series of riddles, winnowing and screening arrive at their destination. Good grain to hired railways sacks, hinderends (small grain) to the farmer's bag for home use and the dirty itchy pulse is blown out under the threshing drum. Two men, including the old boss, handle the grain including weighing, tying, lifting with a hand wound lifting barrow and carried up rickety steps to a trailer.

Another man – the boy or the old man or 'the simpleton' – are in the pulse hole keeping it clear.

I, the threshed straw, walk sedately on straw walkers to the end of the threshing drum and fall into the elevator (or jacker) where I am stacked again by Arthur – "keep the middle up to keep the water out" says Arthur.

If it is a windy day my friends are blown all over the yard and it needs all next day to tidy the place up. I sit in this stack for sometime, but eventually a horse and dray with two men arrive and a load of straw, including me, are carted into the crew yards – full of beef cattle – some is fed to the animals but the great majority of us are used for bedding for two reasons – (a) to keep the cattle clean and comfortable and (b) to make farmyard muck for fertility.

At the end of winter the cattle are sold or turned out to grass and the yards are 3-4' deep in manure.

1953 is just before the front loader and just before tipping trailer and muck spreader, so I am loaded on a flat four-wheel trailer or a horse and cart by hand – fork full by fork full. The trailer then trundles off to the field which is going to be potatoes next year and over a period of days a large muck hill is built. By now I, the humble straw, am feeling rather wet and dirty.

After Christmas, having well rotted and unrecognisable as a straw, I am loaded up on trailers again by hand and on a cold frosty day with sweaty workers and lots of steam I am finally laid to rest on the same field in which I grew. A tractor and trailed single furrow deep digger plough then ploughs me in.

Move on 60 years to 2013.

I am standing in a field of Propino spring barley ready for harvest and expect to yield 15 quarters = 3 tonnes per acre.

On a sunny day a great combine harvester with a 30' wide cutter and capable of doing 60 or 70 acres per day arrives and threshes us at great speed – my grain goes into a big tank, then to a big trailer holding 18 tonnes and is tipped on a drive on floor grain dryer and store.

I, the spent straw am unceremoniously fed into a chopper which smashes me into very small pieces and puts me back where I came from to help with the fertility to grow the next year's potatoes – job done.

Can we now understand what eight farm men on 350 acres used to do?

MARRIAGE AND FAMILY

Margaret

Senior management, the love of my life, and my best friend.

At the time of writing we have been happily married 50 years. We are the product of the Young Farmers Marriage Bureau meeting at the wedding of the late Peter and Sue (Rothery) Lamyman.

The eldest daughter of Jack and Una Fletcher of Blankney Fen and Linwood. She went to Fir Close School in Louth with her cousin Sue, where she remembers 60 years ago on the night of the East Coast flooding gathering in the Head's sitting room to sing 'for those in peril on the sea'. Latterly she went to Queen Margaret's at Escrick Park near York.

She attended a Domestic Science course at Queen's College, Harley Street, staying with her Uncle and Aunt, and then did a Secretarial course at the Lincoln Technical College.

Margaret's first job was working for Penney & Porter, who made farm machinery. She was head hunted to go as Secretary to Philip Gauntlet at Lincolnshire Pheasantries at Mareham Le Fen, where her duties included work with pheasants and partridges and the delivery of day old chicks all over the country.

Father-in-law's prize-winning turnout at the Horncastle Show, 1952.

Billinghay YFC 1961 with all their trophies. For several years they were unbeatable.

She left to work for the Lincolnshire Standard Group. When she announced her engagement in November 1962 she was told it was not worth training her and she was sacked! Something which couldn't happen today.

Billinghay Young Farmers, which she joined, was a formidable club who won everything! Margaret became the Secretary for several years as well as being a member of the Billinghay Quiz team which won everything. The four members

were all cousins – Margaret, Roger Fletcher, Hugh Fletcher and Simon Wright.

I was rather lucky to get her out of the Fen to be my wife!

We have had four homes all within a radius of five miles and lived in three parishes – Canwick, Branston and Coleby.

I missed several important events, including two at the Lincolnshire Show when she was judging the YFC trailers with Richard Grant of Langrick and winning first prize with her sheep. And most important I failed to record Margaret with her First Prize Rosette with her sheep.

Our first home for two and a half years was the bungalow on Canwick Manor Farm at the end of Canwick Avenue, then to a rather badly improved and modernised Canwick Manor Farm House – a

Margaret and her cousin Sue. They have been very close since going away together aged 7.

Nanny doing her party piece of "I'm a little teapot".

Margaret at her 70th Party with seven grandchildren and the family picture she was given.

nice family home with a dreadful bathroom – for two years, then on my father's death a hasty move to Westfield, where all alterations and improvements were done when we had lived there for two years.

During the early years Margaret happily produced four super sons at two year intervals – good family planning but no daughters. *Note:* we have now four super daughters-in-law, so that is okay!

During our married life, Margaret has never 'gone out to work' like the modern wife, *but* has been a great wife and mum, reminder, organiser, planner and 'Mrs Fixit' on the farm. She has also been quite low maintenance, never having smoked and, whilst enjoying a glass of wine when out, has never drunk alcohol at home!

Margaret with our four sons.

In the days before mobile phones, we had a radio system based on the Branston Cooperatives. I was 'ALPHA' Chuck was 'CHARLIE', Tom at Linwood was 'DELTA' and Margaret in the kitchen was 'MRS N'. She has many stories of rescuing other organisations with stubble fires, punctures and breakdowns. We had a lot of laughs at others misfortunes!

Most of our family and friends know of Margaret in the sheep dipper and the 800 escaped sheep on Boxing Day captured forever in two lovely drawings by the late Henry Brewis *see page 50*. Margaret received her bath in the sheep dipper one day in the October school half term. I wasn't there to see it, but apparently Chuck, Bob and A N Other were dipping all the sheep, helped by Margo. In the excitement Margaret got between the bath and a strong willed sheep and in she went. Chuck wanted to use the poy and give her a good

Bentley and Margaret – proud parents with our first-born.

Four boys at Westfield, 1980.

Charles, David and Robert.

Margaret with dog.

Our Silver Wedding.

soaking and keep her in for the regulatory 1 minute. Bob said "what the hell are you doing in there?" Apparently after 600 sheep already through there were a lot of 'currants' in very dirty water.

There are no flies on my wife!

Her attributes are many but no chapter about Margo, as she is known in the village, would be complete without mentioning her huge output at letter writing. The kitchen table from 6.30-7.30am most days is given to writing letters – a splendid trait which has rubbed off on sons and grandchildren.

When the boys were away at school, aged 8-18, she always wrote a good chatty letter twice a week to each of them – no photocopy or carbon paper. All letters from children and grandchildren are kept carefully.

Like a good terrier, once she gets hold of something she wont let go and shakes it until the 'something' is done and sorted.

Remarkably my dear wife has a brilliant relationship with her four daughters in law and seven grandchildren. She has deliberately never commented or criticised and gets teased at Christmas and birthdays when expenditure has to be equal for four sons, for four daughter-in-laws and seven grandchildren. As happy families go, I believe Margo is responsible for ours being high up in the first division.

Over the years we had a farm student most years and a collection of young men working on the pea harvest. Several of whom lived with us. Our kitchen has always been open for visitors, representatives and the farm men, who occasionally needed tea and sympathy after a visit to me in the office round the corner.

In business she has been encouraging and supportive over 50 years – being Company Secretary for as long as I remember and for many years equal partner in the farm partnership. Never pushy but quietly well prepared and full of common sense with family as number one priority.

During our married life she has always been very much involved with her sister Kate, who has learning difficulties, through various homes, secure housing and hostels through to today, where Kate has a superb flat in Sleaford and a wonderful carer, Jan, who Kate loves.

The plaque, now grown into the tree.

The oak tree given by four sons at Will's 21st, 1991.

Additionally, we have had much to do with Dan on and off for 10 years. Our eldest grandson, the product of an unhappy marriage, is now a 21 year old super young man at University reading Business Management. He has a lot to be grateful to his Gran for in so many ways, her attributes of care, patience, perception and persistence have made a smart young man of whom we are all proud.

Eldest grandson, Dan.

Holidays – after a not-too-successful honeymoon in Majorca!, we settled to family holidays at the Lincolnshire, Yorkshire and Norfolk seasides. Usually we rented a house at Sutton-on-Sea during all the years when the boys were little and only wanted sea and sand. Later we had several wonderful years at Watergate Bay, near Newquay, for a fortnight in July before harvest. Quite a performance in those days with no decent road to Cornwall after Exeter, so we went by overnight motor rail from some obscure station in London to St Austell. All the luggage for six of us for a fortnight, including eight sets of fancy dress for two weeks of Ken Stratton's childrens' parties, had to be taken off the roof rack and put in the car. We arrived at St Austell at 6.00 am ready for a relaxed holiday, but had to leave on the Friday night train. Lots of work and packing for mum – but we had great holidays.

The fairy cake challenge – somebody had a great idea to make money for the church and four or five young mums, including Margaret, enlisted a huge army of helpers and got sponsorship of cookers, sugar, flour, milk, etc. The plan was to set up a *Guinness Book of Records* new total for the greatest number of fairy cakes made. I can't remember the numbers, but the village was awash with fairy cakes, with lots of volunteers to put them away. There was also a sort of Nursery school in the church hall run by Margaret and others – no formal training, no rules, and no problems.

One of the cleverest things she did was to find our retirement home in 1999. I had agreed to vacate Westfield by the age of 65, in 2003, in favour of Robert and Sarah, so we decided to go before we were pushed!! We decided that we would like to be in a cliff top village, fairly near all four sons. We had never had neighbours nor lived in a village. Margo found South Cottage at Coleby, which we changed to Harvest Cottage. A lovely stone and pantile cottage with lots of room and commanding views over the Trent valley to Grantham, Belvoir Castle, Newark and Derbyshire on a good day. It can be very windy from the south west. It was in quite good order, but I had been promising Margo a new kitchen for 20 years and a conservatory/sun room. It badly needed a good utility room and an improved downstairs cloakroom with walk-in shower (for our old age), so we set about major changes and one year on were lucky enough to buy the bungalow next door. Before we resold it, we hived off a wider access from the street and most of the garden to erect a three-bay oak and pantile open garage, a fruit frame and some fruit trees, but importantly to secure a potential building site, which could have overlooked us.

In summary, I got it right when I proposed, a brilliant wife, mother, house and home manager, cook and provider. We have been a good team and have had good fortune, good friends and good health to get a lot done with our lives.

Margaret's sheep and land

In 1985 I arrived back from St Bowells with a load of one year-old ewe lambs for summering to produce gimmers including 20 very smart white faced Scotch halfbred ewe lambs which Margaret bought from me with money left to her from her father.

This was the start of a very entertaining period of sheep keeping at Westfield and included expeditions to Kelso Tup Sale to buy the very best (but not too expensive) Suffolk rams. We had Danny, from Ted Albone, Sandy, from Sandy Frazer, and Johnny, from Johnny Wallace in the Borders, who was father-in-law of our Scottish shepherd. That latter ram died after a week! And Danny had a nasty habit of butting one from the rear when you least expected it.

Ewe numbers rose to a maximum of 97, buildings were evacuated in February for indoor lambing and penning. Male lambs were sold fat having been expensively fed for the early market and females were kept to sell as cross-bred gimmers.

Margaret's Suffolk Cross lambs always thrived! They lambed in early February and full of bought feed, the singles and ram lambs went to market where they often topped the market. Eric the wonderful lorry driver who for

Margaret with her two very good rams.

years delivered to market had a great sense of humour and whilst at market worked in the pens marking every lot of sheep with the buyer's colour and marks. He could be relied upon to cheer everybody by saying to the assembled buyers "come on gentlemen, it is the lady's birthday" or "bid up gentlemen, this lady has a difficult husband and a large family".

The female lambs were saved for breeding.

On a visit to the sheep lines at the Lincolnshire Show in 1986, Margaret announced that her Suffolk Cross, Speckled-faced Gimmers were better than anything in the Gimmer class, so next year she entered and won the class! It was quite a performance including careful selection, washing and grooming, staying in a motor caravan on the showground overnight, the presence of Bob with white coat and new halters for judging, etc, as well as considerable activity in researching what was needed and much appreciated and generous help from our friend David Read, who Margaret actually beat in the class – memorable but not repeated!

Richard Bevan, who was Margaret's very pro-active bank manager, used to negotiate grass land rents and agistments with me on behalf of his client, always wishing to charge me excessive values for Residual Manurial Values (RMVs)

Between them they made useful profits which resulted in Margaret selling the flock in 1990 and buying a 10 acre arable field which she called 'Fletchers',

RBN, DMN and Bob Hanson in white coats at the Lincolnshire Show – showing Margaret's 1st prize Gimmer Lambs.

after her father. Several years later she purchased the next door field of 7.5, acres now called 'Jacks', also after her father.

We planted a ¾ acre wood in the middle to straighten a very winding hedge which is called 'Hansons Wood'.

Margaret had a huge stroke of luck with the purchase of 'Jacks'. Within weeks of borrowing money and signing contracts, FINA announced a new high pressure fuel pipeline which went through 'Jacks' from end to end. The owner's compensation plus farmer's compensation for crop loss almost paid for the field – the borrowed money was repaid.

It is interesting to note that Margaret's £500 from her father is now represented by 17 acres of Lincolnshire heathland worth at least £8,000 per acre!

All Saints' Church, Branston

My grandfather Robert was churchwarden for over 20 years at the end of the 19th century. My father, Leethem, was warden for over 20 years in the 1950s and 1960s and I was privileged to be warden from 1969 for 21 years. This was toward the end of the period when Branston had its own vicar – namely the Rev'd Raymond Lucas followed by the Rev'd Brian Stalley followed by the Rev'd Darrol Reagan.

All Saints' Church burned down on Christmas Day 1962, caused by an electrical fault in the organ. Margaret and I had married and went to live and worship in Canwick for five years, so I wasn't involved with the brilliant restoration by George Pace, characterised by the stained glass window, the raised organ and its console, also the steel cross, together with re-located choir, light oak furniture and a light and bright church.

Margaret and I had moved into Westfield Farm in spring 1968 with two boys and number three on the way. This was very soon after Father's death in January. By chance Father's last outing had been to take himself to Branston and bought a house on Lincoln Road next to Park View Avenue, firstly for James and later for Mother.

Mother moved to Branston on the Monday, we moved from Canwick Manor to Westfield on the Wednesday and brother James and Barbara moved from his job at Waddingham Grange to Canwick Manor on the Friday – quite a week! I received a visit soon after we moved in from the Rev'd Raymond Lucas to see if I would be churchwarden! I was churchwarden without being on the electoral roll and ever attending a PCC meeting.

There followed a period of change and improvement.

Firstly we sold part of the field given by the Abel Smith family for a grave-yard extension for the construction of the attractive Abel Smith Gardens – bungalow retirement houses. At the same time reserving a building plot and vehicular access for a new modern rectory for the Rev'd Brian Stalley.

Next we sold our old wooden church hall to the parish of Belchford in the Wolds for £300, where, much modified and improved, it still stands today. After a lot of negotiation and land swaps with neighbours we were able to raise the funds to build the modern stone and pantile hall. The stone came from two old cottages we were demolishing at Potash Yard.

Branston All Saints' Church Hall – built with stone from Potash House and Barn, which were redundant and too near RAF Waddington to redevelop.

Branston Church inside – the magnificent window given by the Abel Smith family.

*Branston Church screen given by Nelstrop
and Howard families, 27th April 1997.*

*Branston Church commemorative plaque
in tower to Robert Nelstrop, Churchwarden
27th April 1897, Queen Victoria's Jubilee.*

To The Greater Glory of God
To commemorate ROBERT NELSTROP
of Westfield Farm, Branston
Churchwarden 1889-1910
In Grateful Memory of
GEORGE LEETHEM NELSTROP
Churchwarden 1945-1959
This screen was given by the
NELSTROP and HOWARD families
on 30th April 1997

For some time I had been aware during the 1990s of a plaque in the tower of All Saints' celebrating the peal of 5040 by a team of local bell ringers on 28th April 1897. This peal was to celebrate Queen Victoria's diamond jubilee anniversary and the giving of an additional two bells by the squire, Alexander Leslie Melville of Branston Hall.

The ringers are all named together with the churchwardens, Alexander Leslie Melville and Robert Nelstrop.

I wrote to all the Nelstrops and Howards and raised enough money to provide the very special oak and glass screen to separate the tower and reduce heat loss, in memory of Robert and Fanny and my father, George Leethem. On 28th April 1997 three teams of bellringers rang. Firstly local worthies rang the same 5040 peal – this was followed by a team from the Cathedral and local area who rang a very special peal – and finally the current team of bellringers, including several learners did a shorter ring. A few days later all the descendants of Robert and Fanny were in church for the dedication, followed by a lunch in the church hall.

Interestingly in 1997 there were 42 descendants of Robert and Fanny from babes in arms up to my mother aged 90. All families were in farming and at a rough guess farmed 8,000 acres from the original 350.

Branston Church Hall, Sunday 4th May 1997, the descendants of Robert and Fanny Nelstrop. To commemorate Robert Nelstrop, Churchwarden 30th April 1897 and the dedication of the new tower screen in All Saints' Church.

The graveyard

Graveyards are a nightmare with curb stones, different headthestones and the fact that after two generations maximum nobody loves and cares for graves – I have very strong feelings.

In the 1980s the farm men, encouraged by the Parish Council, had a serious go at tidying the old cemetery which was closed to burials. We put the good headstones round the outside walls, cleared all other kerbs and headstones, levelled and seeded with the exceptions of one or two big graves and tombs and military graves – it looks quite presentable now and is easily maintained.

Approximately 22 years ago we had a very wet autumn. The Rev'd Reagon called me one day about a problem. He had just had a visit from a very distressed man whose wife had been buried a few months before. On visiting his wife's grave he found a large hole and feared grave robbers. I went to look – there was indeed a huge hole and the coffin could be seen. I sent Robert and some potato casuals with a trailer load of soil from under the potato grader and some wheel barrows. Robert was standing in the hole with just head and arms visible making sure all was well when some ladies walked through the cemetery. They took fright and fled! The soil had been washed out by an underground spring which rose in a wet time. It has never moved again but grew a good crop of potatoes for two years.

Not many funny stories about All Saints' except one fondly remembered…

Arthur Cucksey and the clock

For many years Arthur Cucksey was the very efficient verger and a lovely man. He was born at a time where the squire was churchwarden and everybody knew their place. I attended 8 am Holy Communion on a Sunday when the clocks had changed. Arthur, by now about 75, got out the wine and wafers, handed out the books and got the service going. He then set off up the vertical 15' ladder into the bell chamber and upwards to adjust the church clock. I heard all the whirrings; he came down and went outside to examine the clock. It was obviously wrong because up he went again, more whirring and clanking – down again and through the noisy church door – still not quite right – so up again for a third time – final adjustments – and hastily down the ladder just in time to get to the communion rail, breathless, to receive the bread and wine.

The churchyard

Father planted a beech in the churchyard which has now got very big. When Father died in 1968 with strict instruction for a cremation and no headstone, we were all upset to find out from the crematorium at Grantham (before Lincoln was built) that his ashes had been spread at the crematorium.

In memory I planted three lime trees in a triangle – FAITH, HOPE and CHARITY (love). We nurtured these trees and placed a wreath in the centre every Christmas and Easter. This was a private thing – nobody knew – so I was surprised to find three or four years ago when I delivered the Christmas wreath (by now for Father and Mother) that FAITH and HOPE were gone – only CHARITY (love) remains. I understand and agree with the action taken – CHARITY will now grow to be a very good tree. They left the right one.

'For the greatest of the three is Charity (love).' *I Corinthians 13 v.13.*

The memorial to 1st Para Platoon 250 Light Company RSC, who were in the 'Bridge too far landings' at Arnhem in September 1944.

Arnhem

In 1944 as part of 'Operation Market Garden', which was led by General Urquart from Fulbeck Hall near Grantham, Longhills Hall, the farm buildings and the woodland were requisitioned for 1st Para Platoon, 250 Light Company, RASC of the 1st Airborne Division. A specialist unit of small equipment which was transported to the Dutch landing area in Horsa Gliders whilst the paras parachuted and were much involved on day one of the operation with many of the paras being on the bridge.

The surviving veterans got organised in the 1980s and '90s and had an annual weekend reunion in May. We met and got in conversation at Branston Church one Sunday. They wanted a monument in All Saints' Church, but the Rector was having none of it. Nor was the then owner of Longhills Hall. I offered them a site down the Hall Drive. There is a lovely well-maintained memorial near the B1188 worthy of a visit. At the dedication of the monument, one of the veterans, Ken Clarke, asked if the cowshed was still in the farm yard and if so could he go and look. I went with him and he told me that the 1930 brick cowshed had been the dormitory for 24 men – three per double cow-standing and said "I slept there". The older adjacent building originally the milk cooling plant was baths and showers.

Later I applied for planning permission to convert the cow shed into a four bedroom house – it was originally turned down, but I wrote to Ken Clarke who sent me a wonderful letter about the war and how the building needed to be preserved. I appealed and won and the very nice conversion in Longhills Farm yard is called Arnhem House.

For several years we joined the veterans and their wives on the Saturday lunchtime when we were always 'the farmer and his wife'. We all went to Sunday church and then the party came to Westfield for Sunday lunch before returning home. On one memorable Sunday, one of David's friends Andy Rankin was staying. He is a good pianist and could play all the favourite war songs and tunes. They raised the roof. We exchanged Christmas cards for many years, but 2012 was the first year no card came – *tempus fugit*!

In 1994 the group said they were all going to the 50th anniversary gathering at Arnhem and Oosterbeek and invited us to join them. We went in our motor home, together with our bikes – a wonderful experience. Some events were for veterans only but we witnessed veterans greeting others who they hadn't seen since they were on the bridge – many tearful and moving moments. We parked our van in a glade where all the German Panzer tanks had been hidden and took our bicycles and with 1000's of others on the Saturday cycled out to the heath area where the gliders and paras landed. I have never been in a cycle jam before – and witnessed a re-enactment with several of the veterans jumping.

On the Sunday we watched on TV a very moving parade and church service in Oosterbeek cemetery – rows and rows of immaculate headstones, each with a flower or rose, all attended to by Dutch children and families.

Later we visited the cemetery and I filled my pockets with acorns. I planted them in plant pots on our return and two years later I had an amazing collection of oak species – ordinary, small-leafed, cut-leafed and different colouring. We gave two to the owners of Fulbeck Hall where there was still an untouched room from 'Operation Market Garden', with the walls containing graphs, charts, information and history. Our sons also all had one. These paratroopers were very brave men, wonderful company, full of good stories and proud to be British – we owe them so much.

Gilbert the donkey

Gilbert was a big donkey – he came complete with harness and a cart. The cart was a very primitive vehicle – just a builder's cart with shafts and steel wheels. Gilbert was evil!

When demonstrated, he was immaculate! But in real life he had a mind of his own.

Margaret took him one day to collect the children from Branston Junior School. There was a major incident at the crossroads where he got on the pavement and caused bother. On another day with Margaret he ran away with her and to slow him down she had to steer him into a sugar beet field – much to the amusement of a farm worker. He didn't really stop and Margaret had 200 yards of a very rough ride over sugar beet before he stopped.

That was the end of use by the wife and children, so I took him out one day determined to wear him out and make him do as he was told. We went flat out from Westfield to Canwick Manor, out onto Longlane at the bungalow, down to Mill Lodge pub, where he slowed up enough to turn onto the B1188 to Branston. Again at a canter he went flat out to Branston without encouragement from me. Right at the cross roads to Mere he began to slow up, then it was my turn to put on the pressure, but when we got back to Westfield he was still going well.

I took him out once more, but he had to go.

Dobbin the skewbald and Grandfather's trap

I spent money to restore my grandfather's 1908 rally car – a beautiful trap requiring a very smart cob. The trap, in dark green with black and gold striping, is all original except for the back tail door... one shaft is plated, but it is 'sound as a bell' and complete with upholstery – acetylene lamps, etc.

In a fit of enthusiasm to get going driving, I bought Dobbin. Dobbin was a 'substantial' horse of questionable breeding but he was kind natured and perfect to start.

He came with all harness (a bit heavy duty) and a rubber-tyred four wheel dray. When rigged up in the dray it looked very much like a rag and bone man's outfit.

Despite a few rude remarks in the village, I persevered and when confident put him into the shafts of the rally car. He didn't look right – not quite the ride you would get from a high-stepping smart cob, but we persevered for a while.

More recently Robert and Sarah have had a smart driving pony in the shafts – it would be good to see it used again.

Sons' holiday jobs

All four boys did a three year sandwich course and apart for earning enough in the year out to keep them in beer and petrol, did a job in the Easter holiday.

In several instances there was lambing – mostly at night in such various places as Nottinghamshire, the West Coast of Scotland and the Borders of Scotland. The ones I particularly remember were David at Campbeltown, a rundown old estate with a drunken shepherd, and Bedrule near Hawick where there were 2000 ewes all under cover. When William did a night lambing job, he arrived by arrangement to stay with the shepherd. It was a leap year and the owner had got his dates wrong. After his supper the boss took him round and told him he was on permanent nights. His daughters would help with weak lambs, but he was on his own. He then said "See you in the morning" and disappeared – quite a challenge. Margaret and I went up and stayed in the motor home and I did a night to relieve the boy. There weren't many boring moments with 2000 pregnant ewes, but what a wonderful memory of shed after shed of contented sheep and the noise of new life and fussy mum in the next shed to be visited.

My enthusiasm for sheep and lambing hasn't rubbed off on my lads. The holiday lambings may be responsible for their total lack of enthusiasm for livestock!

The party is over

On New Year's Day 1986, very early in the morning, I sat down to write to my family. We had had a good run farming but I made a mess of the Scottish project at a time when interest rates suddenly went up to 14%. Economies and remedial action were called for! Margaret and the three boys have still got my letter and I am constantly told that the only member of the family who didn't reform was me!

January 1ˢᵗ   1986

To   Mum , Charles , David , Robert , William

Thoughts of 1985 and a message for 1986

THE PARTY IS OVER

1 Christmas Holidays   - Now ended time to get stuck in and Work.
                        - Time also to think of the future and manage our lives

2 Farming   - I have got the message loud & CLEAR — Have you?.

3 As Individuals   - Time marches on - 4 Boys. have all got very.
                         important Exams, and decisions to make.
                        - Mum } The family is growing up, we must
                        - Dad } adjust to their being adults and doing their.
                           own thing.

4 As a family   - The Kids have grown up - Welcome Boys as Friends
A FEW FACTS

We have had the worst farming year for 30 years - I
think we shall lose money for the first time.

I am optimistic about the long term future of Agriculture,
but short term it is all bad news. Those who survive
and are able to expand will be those who can control expenditure
and borrowing

We shall have lost about £100,000 on mercantiles if the
Sale goes through (Probably more if it doesn't) This is my fault.
Probably the only serious mistake I have made in the family.
master Plan. of Expansion, and Setting you boys up in a business
of your choice
Time will tell how serious this is to our family business.
The message for 1986 is extreme caution.

You Boys should all study the history of farming fortunes.
I am concerned you have all chosen farming because you
have seen Mum and Dad having a good life with
plenty of money to spend — you have all been
born and brought up in a period of prosperity.
ARE you ALL PREPARED FOR MAKING A LIVING OUT OF
FARMING WHEN IT IS DEPRESSED; IN DECLINE; AND WHERE THERE
IS A LOT OF HARD WORK FOR VERY LITTLE REWARD ???

PROPOSED   ACTION

THE FARMING BUSINESS
Much reduced expenditure on Capital and New Projects.
Reduced drawings by partners.
Reduced Bank Borrowings
Cut out unnecessary expenditure.
Attention to detail for a Increased Output
                              & Cut out waste.
Sort out Management Structure with Staff Change
Sort out Communications
Much Improved Financial Control, Enterprise Costings + Knowledge of Business

RBN   More Time with Mum and at Home.
        More Time to Think
        Tidy up Memoriskm and Reappraise
        Cut out Personal Expenditure (I must be seen to set a good example)
        Control of Family Expenditure on Drawings, Vehicles Etc.

MUM   Just carry on being the marvellous mum and wife
        . that you are
        Try and Watch the expenditure (mine and yours!)

Boys   Appreciate your mum, your Home, Our Great Family Life
        2 at College — Get Stuck in and WORK.
        2 at School — Get Stuck in and WORK.
        Organise yourselves — Think
                             — Be considerate
                             — your Personal life and your friend
                             — Attend to paper work — Letters
                                                    — Banking + money
                             — Plan your earning and expenditure
        Don't take anything for Granted — Things will change.
        Keep your great sense of fun — Enjoy life to the full.
A NEW YEAR MESSAGE

        I wish you a Very Very Happy, Healthy
        and Successful 1986.

                yours very affectionately
                    Dad.

William in Russia and Poland

In 1992, several years after the Berlin Wall had come down and communism had faltered with the subsequent weakening of Russian grip on the Eastern Block countries, my brother James got much involved in Northern Russia through the Nuffield Foundation of which he is a Scholar.

The Nuffield and Russia project aimed to use World Bank and many other sources of funding available to set up a large Agricultural Education project on a state farm with a magnificent old stately home near Kaliningrad. This is a part of Russia which, as Prussia with wealthy families and wonderful land, was the bread basket of Eastern Europe but had since degenerated to poverty and gross inefficiency with all infrastructures gone.

The master plan needed a very co-operative Estate Manager, which they originally had until he was locked up for fraud!, and aimed to turn the stately home and its surrounding lands into an Agricultural College (rather like the first Farm Institutes after the 2nd World War) and to educate former soldiers who were redundant and other semi-educated and enthusiastic locals.

The project started with the state farm dairy, a huge shed where a large number of women milked by hand, and then to install hygiene and a bottling plant to serve the local town. The first problem encountered was gross inefficiency and very low yields. The reason became very clear. All the locals who lived in poverty and squalor had the legal right to an acre (or was it a hectare?) of land which they could claim and crop annually on the state farm and on it were allowed to keep a cow. So far – so impossible! However, it was

One of several loads of English and European farm equipment which William took to Russia for the Nuffield Russia Trust.

discovered that the peasant's cow never went dry! The number of cows in the herd was always correct but in the middle of the night an old dry cow would be quietly exchanged for a newly-calved young cow.

The farm machinery used to farm the peasants land was all borrowed from the state farm – chaos and wholesale theft.

William joined the project and left England with several lorry loads containing seed, machinery and equipment, grain dryer, tools and materials required for education. I suppose he was a lecturer, technician and demonstrator to people who did not speak a word of English – he quite quickly learned very basic and essential Russian.

Margaret and I had been thinking about visiting him, when out of the blue I had the opportunity to go on a 'trade mission' to Poland on behalf of NIAB, who at that time were very active in training personnel from Eastern Block countries in plant breeding, plant health and certification and generally educating them about the British system acknowledged as the finest in the world.

It had become apparent that it was too expensive to bring over 'bus loads' to Cambridge, so the master plan was to set up a NIAB Centre on a university farm near Poznan and to send NIAB staff to Poland when access was relatively simple and translation much easier. Dr Simon Draper, Deputy Director, with Margaret and I had a very busy three day schedule and were well received including a breakfast meeting in Poznan with the Minister of Agriculture when we had the most wonderful spread of local foods and delicacies and finished up toasting each other and anything else we could think of including the success of our project in vodka, which in many small quantities had to go straight down. I was amazed to see Margaret downing all the vodkas especially at breakfast time. We were also welcomed and entertained by a wonderful colourful autocratic director of the Institute, Professor Bilski. How he had escaped the ravages of communism we couldn't imagine.

Our travelling plans were not simple. There were only two flights per week into Kaliningrad from Copenhagen, so we decided to start with a weekend in Copenhagen, after the weekend we met Simon Draper and flew to Warsaw, having left lots of things William needed at the airport.

After the successful Polish visit we returned to Copenhagen airport to be told that the Scandinavian SAS airlines were on strike! We spent the whole of a Saturday at Copenhagen airport trying to get to Russia and communicating with William. Finally in the evening we got on a plane back to Warsaw from whence we had just come.

Next day we hired a car and drove to a small town next to the Polish/Russian border, where we could drop off the car and we were met by William in his Lada – quite the smartest car around with all the Trabants etc.

The journey to William's house was extraordinary. There seemed to be three lots of border controls. At the first two William smiled and shook hands and we were quickly through, but at the third it was all different. Shortly before getting to the border William stopped the car and put on smart tie and sports jacket and told me to say nothing 'helpful'. At the border there was a huge queue of cars and a few lorries, which William passed and drove straight to the front of the queue. He got out, shook hands with everybody, talked about World Aid, Food Aid, etc and we were through, except that we were taken into a 'chicken hut' and asked to turn out our pockets. I couldn't think why unless it was a case of 'one for me and one for you' but it turned out that we had filled in a document to say what currency we had got. They needed to check we were carrying English £, American dollars, Danish Krona, Polish Zloty and Russian Ruble. It was quite difficult to balance the books! At the time the Russians were desperate for American dollars.

Having negotiated the border it was dark and raining and the roads of old Prussia were bordered by large beech trees and the signs were in Russian as you would expect, except that the 'alphabet' is different, full of Ns, Zs, Hs, etc. The road signs meant nothing. There were no petrol stations (on ration at dedicated stations), no street lights and it was a very good job Will, with two tins of petrol in the back, knew where he was going. If there was a drunk in the middle of the road we were not to stop!

We were made very welcome for a couple of days. A runt pig called *Shashlik* (Russian for barbecue) had been painted with a Union Jack and had been fed scraps for a long time. He had been killed and butchered in our honour by William and we dined on roast pork and sausages. Margaret went off the sausage after enquiring of Will how he had washed the intestine to make the sausage skins.

Shashlik (Russian for barbecue). The runt pig given to William in Russia which the English household fattened up and killed just before we visited.

The area was very interesting, but dull grey and run-down. The lovely land was totally unproductive, using seed of many uncertified generations. The farmyards were full of big heavy machinery, sent in large numbers to the state farms, parked when they broke down and all buildings since communism in town and country were square, concrete and imposing. On the state farm there was one building that was quite different. The Estate

Manager had been impressed with the insulating properties of the 2" deep polystyrene foam in the potato stores, so he had sprayed his house on the outside and cut out the windows and doors. It had turned a brownie orange and all the local birds had tunnelled in to make 1000s of insulated nests!

Flying home was no problem, nobody counted our money to make sure we weren't taking currency out. I had bought Margaret a very good fur hat in the town market but the woman in the shop had tricked us and fraudulently switched it before packing it up for us!

William soldiered on for a while as did brother James and Nuffield. He had ambitions to take on Polish land and I have a file of farms visited, pros and cons and why not suitable – one of the main problems of the day seemed to be that the best ones had gone and that the huge labour force had to be taken on. Those pioneers who were in early have had a hard time but are now having considerable success especially with irrigatable crops and large scale combinable crops.

The Bentley

With a name like mine it could be expected that I would have an ambition to own a Bentley.

The author's 1975 Bentley Corniche. This car was given to him by his three sons for his 72nd birthday.

On the day I left school I made a list of things I wanted to do with my life – as an afterthought I added to own a Bentley before I was 40 (as well as happily married farming 1,000 acres).

The first Bentley I went to look at when I was 19 or 20 was at Gainsborough. John Strange, who went on to become Senior Partner of Hill Osborne Stockbrokers (later to become Brewin Dolphin), who was manager at the time of Neales Gainsborough furniture shop, phoned me about it. The car in question was a vintage Bentley – I can't remember the age and specification, but it was Black Label, strap over the bonnet, hand brake out on the mudguard, etc. It was beautiful – we test drove it to Gate Burton Hall – a bit rough and next to no brakes. The price was £300 and I couldn't afford it. Would it be worth £300,000 today?

Over the years I kept looking and once road tested a secondhand Continental when in Kent, but there always seemed to be more important projects for my money!

It was a wonderful surprise when for my birthday in 2010 my three sons, David, Robert and William, gave me a beautiful 1975 two-door drop head Bentley Corniche in British Racing Green. It is magnificent with a 6750cc engine which doesn't exactly do 20 miles to the gallon. Very special and I am very grateful.

UKF1

From the day I passed my driving test I wanted the registration RBN1. For years in the '60s and '70s I got on badly. I established that BN was a Bolton registration and that BN1 was on the Lord Mayor's car.

Then I saw UKF1 advertised on a Standard 8 in Wales. At the time there was a major fertiliser company called UK Fertiliser (who subsequently went out of business) and I had vision of a big profit!

With my Peugeot 504 estate, I hired a car trailer and set off to the coal mining valleys of Wales. After a search I found the car in a shed on an allotment, paid my money (I think £100) and set off for home. Half way up the steep road leading up to the "heads of the valley" main road, my clutch started to slip and smoke appeared. I was in trouble a long way from home and there was only one way to get out. I vividly remember slowly backing down the hill and through a set of traffic lights into the shopping centre, where I sat for 20 minutes timing the sequence of the traffic lights. At the appropriate moment I set off, doing about 50mph at the lights, and just made it to the top.

Transferring the number in those days was not easy but I took the car on its low loader to the registration office, where much looking at plates on chassis and engine established the pedigree and allowed a transfer.

A fortnight later I saw RBN3 for sale on a Morris 1000 Shooting brake, so off I went to Bolton on a Sunday with the car trailer.

Over the years I have had a tentative attempt to sell UKF1 to the Formula One people and there is now also a United Kingdom Financial Initiative – UKF1.

The Morris 1000 became a banger in which my sons learnt to drive.
However when asked what it stands for, my standard answer is:
UK Farmer   or   UK Father   or   UK Fool
Dear Reader, make your own mind up!

Holidays and the motorhome

Holidays for a working farmer aren't easy to organise when school holidays clash with harvest time and busy periods. With a young family who only needed buckets and spades, we had several years of renting a house with a secure large garden and a beach chalet at Sutton-on-Sea – perfect for children and mum as well as only being 40 miles from home – so that I could 'mix and match' farming and family.

For several years we went to Watergate Bay near Newquay in Cornwall. At the time the road from Exeter to Cornwall was dreadful, so we went by motor rail from an obscure station in London – great fun.

Later we graduated to a single-axle six-berth caravan and had some good holidays with growing family, mainly in Scotland and then when the boys no longer came with us, we bought a motorhome (known as mum and dad's passion wagon!).

The first one on a Mercedes chassis, was luxurious but very slow – we only ever overtook bicycles and tractors – and then we exchanged it for a modern roomy version and visited France, Germany, Switzerland, as well as many trips to lovely places in England, Scotland and Wales. We loved it and very often 'camped wild', staying at lovely isolated spots. One night in the Yorkshire Dales above Hawes, we had found a magic spot and after we had gone to bed, the wind got up and started rocking the van. I can sleep through anything but senior management was anxious and at the third attempt at waking me at 2.00 am to suggest we moved, I jumped out of bed pretty cross, put on my flat hat and drove off the moor to a sheltered spot. Nothing remarkable except that, apart from my hat, I hadn't got a stitch of clothing on. Margaret sat up in bed gigglingat her grumpy husband who eventually saw the funny side.

In later years we increasingly conformed and stayed on very good Caravan Club sites with our dogs.

Happy days!

Our first motorhome.

OTHER FARMING ACTIVITIES

The Co-operatives and pea growing

In 1964, seven very keen young farmers who were all lucky enough to have fathers who let them 'have a go' got together. We never co-operated to save a shilling or earn a shilling, but importantly we joined to do jobs and start enterprises we couldn't do on our own – this is very important! It is also worth recording that we never ever made a decision on the basis of a VOTE. We all agreed or nothing was done; there were some long meetings but we've had 50 years of friendship and business success.

CO-OPERATIVES DON'T MAKE A PROFIT – the members might.

We started with a buying group BH Farming Co in 1964 and quickly moved on to growing vining peas as Lincoln Heath Growers in 1966. This coincided with the end of static viners and the introduction of tractor-drawn mobile pea viners. Self-propelled viners were to follow later.

Considerable grants were available to co-operatives and despite being 30+ miles from the factory, with the aid of a chiller and cleaning site at Branston, we were able to supply chilled product to factories on the east coast.

The machinery was not very reliable; the pea cutters mounted on tractors driven backwards were hard work. The circus of 24 hour a day harvesting with four viners, three pea cutters, mobile workshops, compressors, big water carts and pumps needed a lot of skilled men and organisation to vine 3,000 acres in a 30-mile radius of Branston.

One of my early memories is of a visit to Maidenwell in the Wolds where our pea vining circus had gone to help a neighbouring group. Maidenwell near Louth was farmed by the late Charlie Clark whose farm office was the red public phone box at the top of the farm drive (it is still there!). As a young man Mr Clark had been kicked in the head by a horse and had had a serious repair job to the skull. As a consequence he always wore an 'odd job' metal reinforced bowler hat. I drove down to the yard from the phone box and met this apparition in a bowler and our total conversation went something like this.

"Mr Clark?"

"Yis"

"I've come to look at the pea viners; I hope all is going well?"

"Well it's a pity them cutters ain't made o' wood."

"Oh, why is that, Mr Clark?"

"Well yer cud bon the buggers"

And he stomped off!

There is a lovely story of Charlie Clark with breeches, leggings and bowler walking in to Jack Barclays in London to buy a new Rolls Royce, perhaps apocryphal, but he certainly used to put calves in the Roller at Louth cattle market.

One of my jobs for the pea company was to hire the land each year. With the members contributing up to 1800 acres annually, this got to be quite a task to get up to 4000 acres of good and suitable land in big enough blocks at the right price. I have walked thousands of Lincolnshire acres in many parishes. A pleasurable task and of great interest to me as a practical farmer with a great interest in land and land types.

The shifts changed over on a Saturday day shift. When we were under pressure the directors and farm foremen staffed this for a 10-12 hour shift. In some circles it was known as the 'executive shift', but in others (notably the skilled operators) it was known as the 'wreckers' shift'. The list of accidents and calamities is long. My job was to run the cleaning and chilling line and dispatch lorries. At the time I held a Class four lorry licence (four-wheeler) so when pushed I was dispatched to various factories with a load of tanks of chilled peas. I remember visiting Northray at North Thoresby, Frickley near Doncaster, King's Lynn and several others. On one occasion I found myself on a larger six-wheeler (loaded and ready to go). "Get there as quick as you can" were my instructions. Starting with a steep hill at Normanton near Grantham, this modern lorry was rather different to my old TK Bedford, but we made it, albeit illegally.

I also remember that all the directors used to go to the Moor Lodge Hotel in Branston for a drink after the 12 noon Saturday meeting. I was in the lorry having just delivered a load. After quite a long and entertaining session, I left to join a big family lunch party at Westfield. One of the others (nameless!) left to drive to London to see a girlfriend – all before the advent of the breathalyser.

As well as the buying group, pea growing and potatoes, we also joined to employ an Agronomist, workshop staff and mechanics and a jobbing builder – Brian Lockwood. He was a very useful fellow who could bodge any repair to roofs and gutters, spent a long time at the bookies and loved chocolate cake. He was a very good stone wall builder, but not so good at brick work where a level was required.

Branston Trading Co. – 50th Anniversary

On 29th January 2014 the original five members of the Buying Group Co-operative – Anthony Battle, Chris Howard, Peter Scoley, John Tinsley and RBN – celebrated the formation of the first of a series of co-operatives in January 1964.

We were joined by Simon Wright and Tom Mountain in 1966 to grow vining peas and by Patrick Dean and Stuart Hemington to grow and process potatoes in 1968.

Partners and managers at the 50th Anniversary Celebration.

Along the way we ran a workshop, agrochemical and agronomy department, jobbing builder, etc and the potato company expanded to cold storage, all as cooperatives until we took the major decision to convert to Limited Liability companies.

Just two companies remain – Branston Engineering Ltd run by the Howard family and Branston Potatoes Ltd who are Tesco's largest potato packers with three sites at Branston, Scotland and the south west.

A word on the co-operatives – a great project for seven young farmers with lots of grants available. We all had lots of ideas and it is noteworthy that we never took a vote – always we discussed a proposal (sometimes for a long time) until all agreed or we didn't do it.

A recipe for success and great enduring friendship.

Canwick shed

In the 1970s I was keen to build some storage buildings. There was a problem at Westfield Farm where I was a tenant, so I decided to build at Canwick Manor.

Grants for farm buildings were up to 40% depending on various criteria and there was much building of the 12' to the eaves grain store with 8' walling and gridweld ducts – all of which is now looking very old fashioned, hard work and will soon be redundant.

I saw advertised in the *Farmers' Weekly* 14 buildings, each 225' long x 66' wide x 22' high ex the London Rotherhithe docks, which had been storage buildings for imported timber. I went off to inspect and instantly disliked and distrusted the vendor – an obvious crook who had purchased these buildings to clear the site. He had a brand new red Jaguar and wanted cash up front in return for a lot of promises to deliver to the buyers. I knew that a haulage contractor and a riding school operator had each bought three sheds and lived to regret having paid up front.

I did a deal for three sheds for £5,000 delivered to Lincolnshire to pay 50% up front and £100 per load in cash when loaded on the dock. I knew my vendor couldn't deliver the asbestos in good order and I wanted new anyway. Progress was slow and originally I got loads of steel I didn't particularly want, but cash talks and we got into a pattern of the lorries collecting specific items, stanchions, purlins, trusses, etc when they handed over the £100, and the lorry drivers pocketed the other envelope containing £10.

I never got everything I bought, but finally parted with about £4,000 and had all I required to build the store now standing.

We had piles of steel work over 4-5 acres for a year and at the end sold £1,100 worth of spare roof trusses. Shortly after getting most of what I wanted, I was 'subpoenaed' to appear at the Old Bailey as a witness. My friend with the red Jaguar had purchased 14 sheds from the Greater London Council, but had sold 19 sheds. I attended a meeting of unhappy creditors at the Old Brampton Hut Hotel, now long gone, at the junction of the A1 and A14 in Huntingdon. One man only had purlins, another had roof trusses and another had stanchions – I was the only one with enough of everything to build my shed – what a mess, but I never got to the Old Bailey.

The shed at Canwick, bought secondhand ex-London Dock. Re-erected with new sheeting. The north end is haunted!

We employed father and son Prior from Gravesend in Kent to erect the new building, 2 spans 225' x 66' fitting round an existing 90' x 80' building. They arrived with a caravan and motley selection of cranes, ladders and tools. Money was an issue every Friday afternoon; we had to assess what work was done and what materials were on site. They made a brilliant job of the steelwork and on the Friday after the completion of the framework, Prior had had a large delivery of asbestos sheets ready to commence roofing on Monday am. I obviously paid him too much because I never saw him again!

For several weeks I assumed he would be back but finally we had to get on – another firm of roofers completed the asbestos and metal side sheeting (everything fitted beautifully and I did wonder if all the asbestos would be collected again, but presumably it was paid for!)

This left me with a problem. The yard was full of Prior's equipment, vans, cranes, ladders, paint, etc, which didn't belong to me and I was powerless to move or sell. Eventually the Sheriff's officer was called. We had to prove that Prior owed us money and that his property should be sold by auction to pay off the debt. This solved the problem and cleared the yard.

40 years on it has been a fantastic investment. It originally cost £22,500 after grants. It has stored up to 4,700 tonnes per annum of barley and more recently Robert has converted the building to hold 2,500 tonnes of grain on four-drive

on floors, a 900 tonnes coldstore for potato box storage, and a large covered potato grading and storage area.

That is nearly the end of the story of the timber sheds ex-London docks but not quite – part of the shed (the north end) is haunted. I know not why or how – but over the years dogs have reacted strangely and sometimes there is an odd presence!

Other farms

For several years in the 1960s and 1970s when sale and leaseback was the fashion and with a growing family, I needed to expand. I spent a lot of time in Yorkshire trying to get a farm. I have always had a soft spot for the Yorkshire Wolds together with Scarborough and the East Coast.

Variously we attended auctions and unsuccessfully negotiated on good farms at Foxholes, Langtoft, Thornton Le Dale, Muston near Filey and Wold Newton. With the benefit of hindsight they would have been a fantastic investment, but I was better off with the Linwood Farm later in 1973 and land round home. I found out in 1980, with Mervinslaw, that it is not easy to manage a farm 200 miles away.

Over the years I farmed three farms for one year only; Blankney Fen 550 acres and Stainfield 250 acres were for sale with no buyers and a farm of 250 acres at Reepham where a tenancy didn't materialise as planned. The Blankney Fen farm had been farmed many years before by my later father-in-law, Jack Fletcher, and it was good to farm it. We could have bought it cheaply but my sons didn't want a combinable crops fen farm.

Also in approximately 1990, slightly in a fit of pique, I took over 300 acres of land originally rented for vining peas but no longer required, where I grew harvest peas. Quite a gamble but I had fallen out with a merchant over a seed crop which he didn't want to take at the agreed price and premiums – he told me he would take them at feed value. I said he would not and I drilled them! They were not a huge success but paid quite ok with one big block in Caythorpe low fields and another near Spittalgate roundabout. The logistics at harvest time with two combines, a lorry and two trailers and lots of tractors and trailers were horrendous especially since the only drying and storage we had was at Linwood near Market Rasen. The comments of the Old Somerby farmer when told where we were carting the peas in not printable. 46 miles there and 46 back on a tractor for two loads a day is hard work and a long way.

Mervinslaw

In 1980 flush with cash from a very good potato year, I purchased a 780 acre farm in the borders near Jedburgh called Mervinslaw. It is now a very successful 'open farm' and Deer Park with school rooms, restaurant, nature trails, gift shop, etc.

I had always wanted to farm sheep and cattle and to catch a salmon – I set about it all in a very expensive and inappropriate way. I purchased from Bill Bruce, a gentlemen farmer, who sold because the farmhouse had unfortunately burnt down. He took the insurance money and what I paid him and moved away.

On purchasing the farm, total sales and production came from 1000 store lambs sold from a hill flock and lowland flock, 80 yearling store cattle, wool and hill farm subsidy. Not a huge turnover to support an owner, shepherd, cattle man and tractor man/labourer all living in a lovely row of modernised typical Scottish cottages.

Each year about 25 acres of grassland was ploughed out and sown to 'neeps' – turnips in Scotland and swedes in Lincolnshire. These were grown on ridges and grazed by the ewes in the winter. The land was then sown to barley and undersown back to grass – the barley was all home consumed. I am afraid, with the benefit of hindsight, that I did all the wrong things in the wrong order!

Firstly I should have rebuilt the burnt out farmhouse – all farms need a good farmhouse and its positioning was lovely.

However, we didn't need a farmhouse and were very comfortable in the fourth cottage in the row – "The Bothy", which had been beautifully converted and was ready for us to move into. Upstairs were two bedrooms – our room and opposite a room with Velux windows containing 2 x 2 bunk beds for the boys. Downstairs was a bathroom and open plan kitchen and living room with interesting spiral staircase.

We drained wet land, but I didn't like the way the local contractors did it, so brought up Lincolnshire drainers! We ploughed out old grass land for arable, including a little hill heather and did miles of sheep and cattle fencing with wide gates for modern machinery. We cleared stones, built roads and then in a fit of enthusiasm started building. The original farm steading is on a slope, so a new steading was built. A sheep shed for 720 ewes and a cattle shed, which doubled as grain storage at harvest. We also built individual lamb pens, etc, two very large silage pits together with roads, services, effluent tanks (which weren't a great success) and quite a lot of concrete.

We built up sheep numbers to 900, single suckle cows to 150, 100 autumn calvers and 50 spring calvers, and grew about 200 acres of cereals – wheat and spring/winter barley – and apart from the spraying were equipped to do all jobs ourselves.

1984 harvest was wonderful – huge yields and an easy harvest and we thought we had cracked it – then came 1985. As a committed Christian, I always believed that 'seed time and harvest would never fail'. Seed time was difficult and harvest was an unmitigated disaster – it rained and rained. I remember salvaging blackened and sprouted wheat in November. I believe history repeated itself again in 2008 when again the Borders had a disaster.

It was about this time that interest rates rose to 14% and the economy looked dreadful and many of the reasons for owning and the family enjoying the Borders had gone away. The boys were getting older and no longer wanted to go there in their holidays and Margaret stayed home with them. It wasn't so much fun going on my own, so in 1986 I sold the farm, had a farm sale, packed my bags, dug up an ash tree to replant at Westfield and came home to Lincolnshire with my tail between my legs – I lost money but I don't regret the experience.

The neighbours were very friendly – we made lots of friends and are still in touch with many. At first the local hunting fraternity were nervous of this man from Lincolnshire, who they feared may ban them.

I well remember being invited to a cocktail party at Dolphinston, the home of Sandy and Janette Scott, especially to meet the local fraternity, when I was suddenly aware that I had been gently backed into a large bay window where Charley Scott interrogated me. We finished up the best of friends and we offered hospitality a few months later at the local and traditional riding of the Marches in the wonderful Commoners riding.

Sale and lease-back

Although the practice has now nearly died out, in the 1960s and 1970s there was a huge industry by the Institutions wanting to buy and own agricultural land as part of their portfolio.

Institutional landlords, especially The Crown and Church, have one great advantage; they don't die, so they don't have to sell land to pay death duties.

This was in the days of the old type Farm Tenancies and before FBT's (Farm Business Tenancies). The purchase price paid was usually less than Vacant Possession value. The problem for the Institutional owner is that there has traditionally been a two tier market with tenanted land worth considerably less than Vacant Possession usually about 60-70% of VP value.

I have been involved with this and its vagaries several times mainly with Church Commissioners and Nottingham University, but with several unsuccessful negotiations with Pension Funds, Colleges and Insurance companies.

It was a wonderful way of getting a foot on the ladder and expanding the business with a long term possibility of being able to buy at two-thirds of value, or sometimes to realise a capital gain for retirement.

The family obtained Cross Leys, Wansford, using this method and Abbey Farm, Kirkstead, was purchased from a retiring tenant.

Farm grants and subsidies

After the war when extra food production became vital, the farmers were paid subsidies for various activities in the pursuit of productivity, land and building modernisation and improvement.

Variously in the period 1960-1990 we received monies for:

Ploughing out grass

Lime and application including beet factory waste lime up to 40%

Drainage up to 40%

Shed building and driers up to 50%

Roads

Irrigation ponds and underground mains

Hedge removal and field size enlargement

I don't think anybody ever mentioned conservation of either wildlife or land until approx 1980 when the emphasis changed from food production (there is supposedly lots of cheap food in the world without UK growing it) to increasing emphasis on wildlife, hedge and trees and energy.

It is important to differentiate between farming subsides and social subsidies. Much of the very beautiful upland area of the UK needs a well-populated countryside managed for agriculture and tourism with enough people to support schools, hospitals and the social structure of the area. This is often called a farming subsidy – it is not.

AWAY FROM THE FARM

Auctions and farm sales

I love an auction – the excitement and suspense is gripping – whether or not there is anything one wishes to buy or sell.

I learnt a valuable lesson when a teenager. I had gone with Father to the Annual Lincoln Red Cattle auction which was held on the Carholme Racecourse at Lincoln with all the bulls tethered in the racing stables. A bull was being sold when I waved to my friend Rob Smith whose father was a prominent breeder. My bid was taken, down came the hammer and for a few embarrassing moments I was the proud owner of a Pedigree Lincoln Red bull.

I also learned that it was very easy to come home from farm dispersal sales with a load of rubbish or things that didn't quite work. As a boy I went with Father to a sale in Lincoln where the Co-op, having moved their dairies out of town, had decided to do away with all their horses, floats and assorted items. I can't remember anything about the horses but there was an amazing display of harness, brasses and accessories. We landed home with lots of them – very cheap but at the end of the horse era probably never used – we should have bought all the brasses!

Father, who had survived during the great Depression when many of his friends and neighbours went bankrupt, told me that there was an unwritten rule that one should always attend and buy something at a neighbour or friend's sale. I have the sale particulars of 'The late Alderman Laughton Harvey' of St Johns Farm (now Manor Farm), Bracebridge Heath on 23rd March 1932, conducted by Joseph E. Walter & Son, Auctioneers and Valuers, 10 Bank Street, Horncastle.

My father was an executor to this neighbour – a bachelor Gentleman Farmer. It is interesting that purchasers included Nelstrop, Neesham, Battle, Pears, Wilson, Burtt, Gambles, Chennells, Cartright, Meanwell, Bembridge, Applewhite, Theaker, Ward, Sheldon, with pigs bought by Curtis and cattle by Pepperdine. Many of those farmers are still going strong as well as Walters the Auctioneers, Curtis Pork Butchers and Pepperdines Butchers.

Father bought:	12 sheep troughs	£6.00 (new money equivalent)
	Set of harrows	£2.50
	Sheep dip and medicine	£1.50
	10 hoggets x 2	£20.00
	1 heifer	£19.00
	4 steers	£74.50
	3 calves @ £7.50	£22.50
	Grey mare ('Tulip')	£26.00

From this 400 acre tenanted farm the sales summary was (old money)

Implements	831	5	6
293 sheep	860	0	6
13 pigs	42	12	0
83 cattle	1469	15	0
12 horses	362	10	0
TOTAL	3566	3	0

The horses names are interesting – Short, Jolly, Bute, Bonney, Captain, Jet, Traveller, Violet, Blossom, Beauty, Tulip plus an unnamed pony.

As a keen young farmer I was keen to expand the 350 acre farm business and never missed a farm auction, which for years were at 3.00 pm on Fridays at Lincoln Corn Exchange. Farmers and trades people, from Corn Merchants to Cattle medicine salesmen to Auctioneers to various other sellers and buyers of essentials to the farming fraternity gathered at 1.00 pm to do business. Many farmers carried cheque books and unpaid bills and in the space of one or two hours paid their bills and ordered all their requirements. The banks closed at 3.00 pm, so all wages cash had to be collected before or after the Corn Exchange. Some farmers and trades people would go to the club or pub – the rest of us did our shopping and went home!

I have several memories of odd occurrences at the auction. Henry Morris, an Auctioneer, who liked a pink gin with his lunch was in full flow selling a farm when he lost his way and started again £100,000 less than his last bid. After a bit of tittering and leg pull he got there in the end.

Blackmoor Farm at Aubourn was definitely sold to the wrong man. The last two bids came from Major Sir David Hawley from Jas Martin & Co buying for F. G. Battles of Potterhanworth, and Robert Coy of Charles Sharpe and Co of Sleaford who had a plant breeding station at Boothby Graffoe. The last bid definitely came from Sir David but the farm was knocked down to Robert Coy. Sir David was very deaf from his appalling war experience in Burma. Consequently he didn't challenge and by the end of the day when both parties went to sign and pay it was too late.

We had a useful local farm – Hall Farm Dunston – for sale by George Mawer & Co in about 1970. Several of us had got excited to various degrees. Derek Mawer tells the story that 10 minutes before the auction the late Eric Parker of Blankney approached him and said 'Good afternoon Mr Mawer, I am here to buy this farm, where would you like me to sit?' and of course he bought it!

The various members of the Branston Co-operatives got a reputation for getting their act together over land sales, for example, the Branston Co-op land was split four ways with two other boundary adjustments. We were known as the 'Branston Brethren' by some of the Lincoln Auctioneers.

When Harry Woods of Beaufoe Manor Bracebridge Heath died, the farm was sold by auction. The two neighbours wanted to purchase and split it down the middle. I was representing Battle & Pears to the south and went in to Lincoln on the morning of the auction to read the contract details and small print. I first met the late David Walter, who was confident of much interest and a good price. We had a small wager of a new £1 note on its sale price – he went high, I went low – surprise, surprise! I then left David and found the young lady who would show me the contract. In conversation I discovered that I was the first person to look! After an interesting cat and mouse auction we purchased it. I still have the 2 x £1 notes, David's and mine.

Probably my most profitable auction purchase concerns 40 acres owned and for sale by Trent Regional Health Authority. When I was a boy the Lincoln Hospitals farmed and produced food for the hospitals. Bracebridge Heath was the headquarters with vegetables and livestock, all waste food was boiled and fed to the pigs (together with a few spoons and forks!) which in turn fed the patients. There was a nucleus of farm workers but most of the work was done by the patients. I remember one or two. There was a lovely man who had caught his arm in a machine at Hopper Bicycles of North Lincolnshire. He never stopped talking – no sentences just phrases and words. Very sad as were most of the cases. I also remember an old boy who pushed his barrow very enthusiastically but upside down – nobody filled it!

The 40 acres adjacent to the hospital and next to our Canwick Manor Farm was for sale by public auction. It was a nice field and the first for sale next to home. I was determined to buy it!

On the morning of the auction I went for a good walk round, inspected the boundaries, etc. I came across a grassy uncultivated area in the middle and further investigation found two cast iron tops which I couldn't move. I went home and came back with a long bar and torch etc and got a lid off. Inside was a huge beautifully constructed brick domed hole – big enough to take two double decker busses! This was not mentioned in the particulars.

I telephoned Tom March the Auctioneer who had no idea about the hole – I said I was going to ask at the auction. Just before I left for the auction he phoned back – it was a redundant flood water soakaway and was to be sold with the field – fortunately I asked for this in writing! At the auction my carefully laid plans to 'buy off' the neighbours were scuppered by Fred Lilly of Waddington who had just sold some building land. At a public auction you keep bidding or don't buy. I kept bidding and did buy it.

Several weeks later the papers came for the final exchange and a new clause about 'existing services and facilities' had been inserted. My enquiries revealed that 'the hole' was not redundant and was a strategic part of the surface water drainage of the Hospital site. There followed some interesting negotiations over 'the hole'. I offered to sell it back for what I thought a new one would cost which would have cheapened the purchase price considerably. The District Valuer representing the Public Authority vendor said 'No'. In turn I said 'no – move your hole onto your land'. Several weeks later I espied much digging over the boundary and went to see the Irishman in charge. There were lorries carting the hard core away, so I suggested to Paddy that for a tenner he might like to bring his digger and take the top off the vault and then save lots of money by putting the hard core in my hole. This was duly done and all signs of 'the hole' disappeared. This area is now houses so whether the builders managed to avoid two large soakaways I don't know.

The last time I tried to buy land at auction was about 18 years ago, when William was about ready for a farm. There was a very nice farm at East Barkwith near Wragby with a lovely house. The master plan was for David to farm combinable crops and William to grow potatoes and other irrigatable crops on Linwood and the new farm – five miles apart. I went well beyond my limit but it was bought by Hugh Bourne, the builder. I congratulated him after the Auction – "Aye" he said, "I was going to buy it – I have another three million to get into land." I replied "Please let me know when you have got it spent." Subsequently he sold his building business for many, many millions. He and his family now own and farm over 12,000 acres – all from a standing start – what a wonderful man who has used his money to support Lincolnshire Agricultural Society, Lincoln Cathedral and the Prince's Trust, and other good causes.

Scottish seed potato trips

When we established the Potato Co-operative, one of the priorities was to much improve our seed potato source and the quality and size grading of the seed. four of us set off in my Peugeot estate and as 20+ year olds were right loyally entertained by Major Pat Henderson, Guid Rutherford, Wyne Colville and Roy McLean. We went into field after field of immaculate seed potatoes, then ate and drank at 'Kings of Kinloch Hotel'. With sore heads we reported at Guid Rutherfords on the second morning and, after an alcoholic and hospitable morning looking at yet more super crops, we arrived back at the hotel for lunch before driving back to Lincolnshire.

Orders were taken and soon a very pretty waitress came with the tomato soup and promptly poured a bowl into Anthony Battle's lap. He says it was very hot – all I remember was that our happy party insisted she mopped it up with a very embarrassed Anthony and a more embarrassed waitress.

This was before the days of breathalysers – I drove home.

Farms and crop judging

I was asked three times to judge crops for the Suffolk Agricultural Society, an organisation who took this very seriously. As well as the traditional farm judging with prizes for conservation, Suffolk had prizes for each crop. First time I judged winter barley, then spring barley and finally beans. I had a local minder who drove me round and gave me tea when we had finished. I gathered that some judges rode round and judged from the car and gateway, but I enjoyed my day, striding round field after field of outstanding crops. My biggest problem in year one was deciding between the obvious heaviest yielding field with lots of wild oats and an immaculate crop of moderate yielding high quality malting barley. The heavy crop would make the most money but I gave first prize to the immaculate crop.

I stewarded for several years the Lincolnshire Agricultural Society competition for Farm and Conservation. This was a good competition, the standard of farms was as important as the efforts at conservation in all its forms. After several years I decided that our farm was as good as most, so I entered the competition and shared the award in 1990 with my good friend Anthony Battle of Potterhanworth.

Committees and appointments

Over the years I spent a lot of time on various committees. It is hard to quantify what good and what changes occurred as a result of my efforts. Until later in life when I did a few consultancy jobs, nothing paid a fee, so the cost in time and mileage was probably enormous, however I enjoyed it!

I farmed through a period when I had two foremen and 5-8 farm men and could be away for days at a time. My sons, however, have few men and much of the time run their business from the tractor or forklift seat with a mobile phone and all the latest technology.

In the early days of marriage I was involved with the:

NFU – Chairman of local branch, Chairman of Potatoes at county level and Syndicate Credits – an organisation for NFU members financed by Midland Bank for very favourable purchase of machinery.

School Governors – local infant school, a job I was never comfortable with.

Garrets Charity – very little distributable funds but owned a 2.4 acre field at Fulbeck 70 yards wide on escarpment – steep – sloping at top – wet at bottom – landlocked and generally not good! I was able to sell this after several years of difficult negotiations.

Lincs. Agricultural Society – I was on the board for two or three years when conservation was becoming trendy and helped establish a wildlife pond as part of the woodland and conservation exhibit (the pond always leaked!).

For many years I was a steward of sheep shearing. We had an open competition on the first day and Young Farmers and demonstration on the 2nd.

The Lincolnshire Show has a fine reputation for dress and smartness and whilst we sheep stewards didn't wear a bowler, we did turn up with best suits and ties, etc. The problem was the sheep and their greasy wool. First job on the first day was to handle all sheep to arrive at a situation where each competitor's pen of two sheep were equal, especially wool on the belly and legs, no dry patches and similar-sized sheep. Although we took off our ties and donned boiler suits we always landed up at the Vice Presidents for breakfast at 9.00 am feeling very greasy, sweaty and uncomfortable. The other big problem was that I had no time to accompany Margaret to lunch and around the show. Something had to change, so I was delighted to change to the Conservation area where in the very early days of farmer awareness the LAS set out to educate and enthuse. I believe we did a good job and the area is now huge and very well supported. Much later having retired from duty, Margaret and I were pleased to sponsor the Epic Centre.

FWAG (Farming and Wildlife Advisory Group) – The late Tony Mardon of ADAS phoned me and asked if I would chair a new committee. It was a mixture of land owners (Lord Yarburgh and Lt Col Sutton Nelthorpe), farmers, conservationists, etc including the long hair and sandals fraternity. Not easy but slowly and surely we started to make a mark including an impressive display at the Lincolnshire Show. The organisation went on to handle grants and do a great job.

The East Midlands Agricultural Regional Panel – I really enjoyed the job. It was non-political and we met up to three times a year to discuss the problems of the moment and the Chairmen of the four or five regional panels had regular meetings with the Minister of Agriculture. A very good system which was scrapped by the last Labour Government when they came in. I travelled to these meetings with Ted Grant of Old Leake and the late George Henry Parker – an education in itself.

Our Chairman was the late Sir Sydney King, President of the Farm Workers Union. A splendid man with his own beliefs for a Utopian Society, but much respected by all. I remember a panel outing to Boughton House in Northamptonshire when the owner – the paraplegic Duke of Buccleugh – drove us round his estate. I listened fascinated in the back, whilst the Duke and Sir Sydney argued the morals and practicalities of the estates provision of modernised housing for his workers. The Duke was justifiably proud of all his housing. Sir Sydney considered the workers should be able to buy their houses – two splendid men in earnest debate.

The LaDiDA – The Lincoln and District Dinner to Agriculture. Having been on the committee which organised the Fatstock Dinners held after the

Christmas Fatstock Show at Lincoln, it was good that a small enthusiastic team resurrected the dinner after the market closed and christened it the LaDiDA. A male-only dinner which has changed over the years, but essentially has a key speaker with a message who replies to the Toast of Agriculture and a funny/rude speaker who replies to the Toast of the Allied Traders and Professionals. After a rather dodgy involvement with proposing allied Traders when I harangued the Lincoln butchers for being mean, I was asked to be president in 1986 for three years, at a time when the dinner was at the Moor Lodge Hotel at Branston. I remember we had a politician who was in a hurry to speak and get back for a crucial vote in the House of Parliament and a well know economist Michael Murphy from Cambridge University, who arrived late and breathless, got his notes mixed up and started in the middle and finished at the beginning! However we had some very funny speakers and very good beef.

CARAS AND FRAgS – After many years involvement at NIAB I was very pleased to be asked to become an Associate of the Royal Agricultural Societies and a few years ago to be made a Fellow – FRAgS. The Council for Awards of Royal Agricultural Societies operates separately in England, Scotland, Wales and Ireland and acknowledges those male and female who have made a valuable contribute to agriculture in farming, science and research, conservation, pioneering, marketing, etc etc.

The English Fellows and Associates meet at least twice a year, the main date covers the AGM and visits over two days with a summer visit later in the year. The moderation panel who make the awards acts somewhat like a secret society – nobody is asked if they want to join. After a period of secret research the 'chosen' are written to and asked if they would like to join – newly elected Associates are then included in the newsletters together with their inspirational activities.

Consultancy and management

In my early 20s I was asked by the late Nancy Battle, mother of Jane Carmichael, to farm and manage **Battle & Pears Ltd – Glebe Farm,** Waddington Heath – 235 acres wheat and barley, sugar beet and potatoes, cattle, sheep and pigs with a labour force of four living in the two cottages. The hard winter of 1962/3 with no water supply for six weeks was very difficult and hastened the demise of the cattle and pig enterprises. With increasing mechanisation and reduced labour our two organisations shared specialist equipment and both entered into the various cooperatives at the same time and committed men and machinery. With the owners being away abroad, but with recourses for expansion, this was a time of expansion, with land at Waddington, Navenby, Heydour near Grantham and half of Beaufoe Manor next door split with Patrick Dean bringing the total to 450 acres. This arrangement ended in 1990 when David and Jane returned to England, but we continued to share and work together for some time.

Tumby – I was phoned by my good friend Roger Spurrier of Jas. Martin & Co. and asked to have a look at the Tumby Estate, who were not getting the results expected. I spent a lot of time on the farm, with the Manager and examining the books and farming systems. I presented my report for actions and was asked to meet the owner to discuss. I was subsequently asked to stay on and make all my recommendations and changes work. I agreed with the proviso that the Shoot Manager must control the rabbits and the Farm Manager must go with my recommendations. Three days later I got a phone call from Roger to say that the owner had met his Manager and Shoot Manager – neither would work with me, so would I please send my bill and never set foot on the estate again! I was sacked before I had started! Roger was kind enough to say a few years later that I had stirred things up. My report had been acted upon and all was well. He also much later asked me to shoot on the estate, so I have been back. I was content with the decision particularly that the owner would not do anything to upset the Shoot Manager, who I am reliably informed served with him in the war and saved his life.

Rauceby – Another consultancy job where I didn't last long. Mrs Jillian Hoare had unexpectedly inherited the Rauceby estate – a mixture of in-hand and let farms. Rationalisation was taking place. I was asked to advise and help manage. I much enjoyed this but the estate had a very good working Manager called Richard Ward. After a year I sacked myself, Richard was doing a great job – he is still there.

Hainton – My last advisory job (as an employee of Jas. Martin & Co.) was an eight year stint with the late James Heneage at Hainton. I very much enjoyed the man and the job. I was responsible for cash flow budgets, cropping, single farm payments paper work and applications for two businesses, liaising with the agronomist, general farm advice and attendance at all Business and accountancy meetings. My Achilles heel was my competence (incompetence) with the computer. Sarah Green, the farm secretary, used to get me organised and tell me which buttons to press. I spent hours longer than I should on monthly budget comparisons and print outs and never sent in a bill for a lot of the hours spent. At least I used to get correct answers! James worked very hard and was a great enthusiast. I had to be very careful with my advice and not think aloud until sure – things were acted upon immediately.

I retired aged 67, when I was given a very handsome leather briefcase, which is much used. On the way home that afternoon I thought, ok I have retired, what to do next and what not to do again? I decided there and then never to touch a computer again. I never have! I don't do emails, texting or internet banking. I am NOT proud of it, but with a good secretary I have just got away with it!

My last job at Hainton I consider my most successful. For sometime I had advised James that he needed a full-time manager to allow James and Roberta to travel more and spend more time on the development of the estate. This was agreed upon and I was asked to be involved with this new appointment. I met the several promising applicants for an hour before they were interviewed by James and Robin Battle of Jas. Martin & Co. The ultimate successful applicant, John, was older and more experienced than the others and I well remember he asked a lot of good searching questions including "Is this estate solvent?". What a good question – I assured him it certainly was and later back in the office told James that the man wanted £10k more than budget, but he was the one. Eight years later, James has passed on and young Christopher is the new squire, with John firmly in charge and much liked and respected.

National Institute of Agricultural Botany (NIAB)

I was privileged and proud to have been involved at NIAB for almost 30 years from 1983 until 2012. Having been a member of the Minister of Agriculture's East Midland Regional panel for several years, I was invited to become a Member of the Council of NIAB as a MAFF appointee. There were 26 members of Council representing farmers and agriculture, seed trade, MAFF, millers, brewers, etc. and generally represented by the great and the good! It was a privilege to be on Council and a committee that gave 'job satisfaction'.

I quickly found myself a Member of several TAC's (Trial Advisor Committee) Cereals, Sugar Beet, which I attended for the last time in 2012 and Potatoes which I most enjoyed. The farming industry was supplied with a recommended list for all crops by NIAB – the TAC's debated all new varieties, their attributes and failings and made a new annual list, which had to have the approval of Council.

There were only every three chairmen of the Potato Committee (PTAC), Messrs Kendall of Norfolk, Eric Lister and myself. It became increasingly difficult to fund and produce a recommended list. The packers, supermarkets and processors of chips and crisps all had their own varieties and needs and the Recommended List was abandoned in 2002. A list of varieties is still produced annually for everyone to make up their own mind. The potato is so complex with earlies, mid crop and lates, white and yellow flesh, dry matter, bruising, storing, disease and blight.

Unlike all other crop lists which measured yield and productivity and noted crop characteristics and disease susceptibility, the potato list was all about quality and characteristics important to the user and housewife. Yield grown in the field had little correlation to yield of the right size, good skin colour, good taste and no internal defects.

Sugar beet (SBTAC) on the other hand has a very simple aim – sugar. In the 26 years I was on the committee, there has been a spectacular increase in yields and sugar content. Most credit must go to the plant breeders, pelleting of seed with chemical treatments in the seed, and emergence and disease control and the research in disease, weed control, virus yellows, bolting, etc. A good yield in the 1980s of 16 tonne/acre at 16% sugar is now 30 tonne/acre at 18.5% sugar. The plant breeders have changed the shape from a fat parsnip with a flat top to a deep rooted slim mangold shape full of sugar with bolting and disease resistance. Germination of 90% is now the norm compared with 70% and 80% in 1983.

Getting back to NIAB, I was Vice Chairman of Council in 1996 & 1997 and Chairman in 1998 & 1999. Things were a changing and it was time to take NIAB private as the government were wanting out of research, testing, seed legislation, etc. After prolonged negotiation a group of five representatives from NIAB met a team from MAFF in London on January 20th 1998 and finally agreed a formula and a deal. We seemed to spend all afternoon dotting i's and crossing t's and then changing it all until at 5.00pm we broke up for a wee break and to phone home (I missed

RBN as Chairman of NIAB Council 1998.

the LaDiDA dinner) and to have each team in separate rooms for 20 minutes.

In the loo, David Boreham of MAFF said he thought we would have to meet again – I said 'Like hell we would!" I was here to sort it however long it took (I don't like London!). When I got back to our room, Tim Lawson of Bidwells , who negotiated brilliantly for NIAB was very 'laid back' – "Don't worry" he said "They are instructed to do a deal and Civil Servants don't work overtime – it will be all sorted out by 6.00pm." We were all agreed and finished by 5.50pm!

Footnote: With the passage of time it is easy to see what a brilliant move this was. John Macleod and the team put NIAB on a firm footing for the future. The redundancy fund worked well, government long term contracts gave us a good start. All the staff having been Government employees have a Civil

NIAB Board sealing documents to transfer from a Government sponsored organisation to the private sector. Note the wonderful company seal.

Servant type pension. The only problem is that along with other organisations NIAB has a large pension deficit, somewhat dissipated by the ability to sell building land in Cambridge.

In 2001 when my final stint on NIAB Council was up, I attended a small farewell celebration when kind words were said and I left NIAB I thought for ever, but that wasn't the end.

In 2002 I was invited back to be a member of the NIAB Trust as part of restructuring. NIAB Ltd did the work and NIAB Trust owned all the assets and property and there was an 'interesting' portfolio of property some owned outright and some jointly owned with MAFF. At this time, Cambridge needed more houses, there was the start of negotiation and planning changes which culminated in sales of land for housing for a lot of money. There was also the question of relocation of NIAB to be addressed and I looked at several other locations and opportunities within the Cambridge postal code (CB).

Quick promotion to Chairman of the Trust followed in 2003-2006. We had a great panel of trustees several of whom couldn't be Chairman for several very good reasons. However I was privileged to work with a very good team who, despite delays in what we wanted, achieved much for the future of NIAB. I was succeeded by Professor John Macleod, the ex-CEO of NIAB and a great friend to NIAB and to myself, with exceptional talent with a scientific background, but also practical and wise.

There has recently been a lot of publicity in the press and on television about a wheat breeding programme at NIAB where the scientists have gone right back to the grass species from which wheat came several 1000 years ago and are breeding up a completely new strain of wheat (not a GMO!). Early indications give a massive yield increase. I am pleased to have been a member of NIAB Trust which debated and agreed to fund this research.

When I retired in 2008, I discussed with John an award for NIAB staff and between us we came up with an annual award for 'Enterprise and Innovation'. John's wife Janet was a sculptress of some renown working mainly in bronze and she produced for me 22 medallions – one for John, one for me and 20 for the annual award for the next 20 years.

The winners so far have been:

2009 Sue Arnold – who revolutionised accounting and reporting procedures to be a) accurate and b) easily understandable.

2010 The Artemisia Team – recognition of work on the wormwood plant resulting in significant increase of yield of anti malaria remedy which will ultimately benefit malaria sufferers worldwide.

2011 NIAB Transformation Team – Andy Greenland, Emma Wallington – to recognise the team efforts in driving the transgenic initiative forward, writing new controls and making the NIAB team one of the best regarded wheat transformation teams in the world.

2012 NIAB Innovation Farm – Lydia Smith and team – recognised team effort in innovation and making Innovation Farm a nationally recognised brand.

2013 Ron Stobart – Amalgamate NIAB & TAG and securing substantial funding.

It was a sad day but a great privilege to give one third of the eulogy concerning NIAB and his service to agriculture at John's memorial service. I followed a villager and the past Chairman of RHS (Royal Horticultural Society). John was Chairman Elect of the RHS when he died – a great man.

SPORTING ACTIVITIES AND DOGS

Country sports and sporting dogs

I have often wondered whether it is the 'thrill of the chase' or the 'satisfaction of pursuit and kill' or the 'chance to get close to nature and to enjoy all that is good about the countryside' or the 'company of good friends and like-minded people together with the generous hospitality that goes with it'.

In my young days I tried my hand at rabbiting with ferrets, pigeon shooting, coarse fishing and occasionally riding a horse, but never to follow hounds.

Over the years my love of game shooting has given me a lot of pleasure. I make no excuse for the fact that I belong to a privileged group of a few farmers who ran a good shoot, invited their friends and enjoyed those same friends hospitality at their shoot. I was never a good shot compared with many friends and acquaintances, but 'every dog has his day' and I still fondly remember exceptional shots, drives and days and, never one to subscribe to the numbers game, my perfect day is partridge shooting with good company and hospitality in a bit of Lincolnshire where the terrain and the weather combine to make the birds fast, high and difficult – one remembered is better than a dozen flappers on a sunny windless day. This perfect day (of which I am lucky to have had several) includes the company of my dog. I feel incomplete without one at my side and get a lot of pleasure from picking up – both after a drive when I was shooting and now when I am privileged to go picking up.

I have had a collection of 'character' dogs – several could have been brilliant if only their owner and handler had been competent and consistent. Perhaps we deserved each other. From a collection of great family dogs when the children were young, I graduated to two wild Springer spaniels, but my love of black Cocker spaniels began 20 years ago when son David arrived home from college with a highly-trained kennel dog, an 18 month old bitch, called Sooty. Her owner Louise Nickerson, also at college couldn't manage her, so we had her on approval for a week. She shot into the house and jumped on the kitchen table. She was not house trained, had no social graces, but was immaculately trained to the whistle and hand controls by a very well known breeder and trainer, Lindsay Waddell. I just couldn't be shouting "Sooty, Sooty" across the fields of Lincolnshire, so

Sox (formerly known as Sooty).

quickly changed her name to Sox. She learned very quickly, but she also learned how to chase a hare. We had a lot of fun and several of my friends used to invite Sox to their shoot and me to come with her!

I was shooting with her at Welton le Marsh near Spilsby when she was about 5 years old when a picker-up with several Cockers and a black Labrador came to me and said "excuse me sir but I think I have seen that dog before but not in Lincolnshire. Her name is Sooty and she has a brother called Sweep. She was bred by Lindsay Waddell from Raby Castle. Sooty was given by Sir Joseph Nickerson to his daughter Louise and I saw her on a grouse moor with Louise." I was amazed at this man's knowledge and tried to throw him by telling him that her name was Sox, but as an expert dogman he was sure about her breeding and pedigree. A very special moment on a day's shoot.

On the same shoot but a different year, I was phoned by the host Rob Smith and asked to collect the late William Epton from his home and to look after him. What a lovely man – who called everyone by their surname – an extrovert Lincoln solicitor who during the journey to the shoot knew who owned every field between Lincoln and Spilsby and was full of great stories.

During the day 'Father William' kept losing things. He lost his cartridge bag, gun sleeve, trousers (that took a bit of sorting out) and finally his glasses during a drive. At the end of the drive all the beaters were collected up and a yard apart beautifully executed a 'Father Williams glasses drive' when 'that which was lost was found' with much rejoicing.

Game shooting

I am not very proud of the fact that until 2013 I have never paid directly for a days shooting! However, I daren't calculate what my chosen sport has cost me and my business.

I have spent wonderful days with wonderful friends in wonderful bits of England and Scotland, mainly shooting partridges, pheasants and a few grouse. I have been asked but have never shot with double guns. One is more than enough for me and I have never been interested in the 'numbers' game. One memorable bird is worth a dozen instantly forgotten.

The Westfield shoot has given a lot of pleasure to the family, friends and guests. In its various forms with various neighbours it has matured to today when with help from the neighbouring game keeper, Raymond Shipley, Robert (now in charge) puts on six days a year specialising in partridge – mainly French but a healthy smattering of grey legs. No commercial lets and all done with family and friends for fun.

I must acknowledge our farm neighbours who do not poach or feed on boundary – we all work together – consequently our returns % is exceptionally

The Shooting Gazette, February 1999. Robert's Stag Party.

Family shoot, 30th December, 2010. This picture includes all the Nelstrops, except Charles in Canada.

high. I also acknowledge the early work done by Bob Hanson, a great countryman with infinite patience with broody hens and part-time keepering between his other jobs.

Talking numbers for a moment we would aim for a 150-180 head day. The (accidental) record is 356 with a few days over 200 and many especially at the end of a season under 100.

Three of my four sons are keen shots (better than I ever was) and we have had great days over 40 years starting with the Godfathers' shoot when their eight Godfathers shot and the boys were bush beaters through to the boys' shooting with their Godfathers' supervising, then each boy given a day to entertain his friends (all under supervision) etc.

In the early days with joint shoots, the farm men were the bush beaters, some keener than others. There was an unfortunate occasion when I lost my temper with the beaters – our employees *and* our neighbours' men – next morning I was in their yard at 7.00 am to apologise and I never again shot at home, except occasionally on the tidy up day at the end of the season. We then graduated to RAF personnel moonlighting. On one foggy day they heard shooting and followed it – they were found near RAF Waddington. Then we had a number of police and the current dedicated team is made up of mainly retired (some husbands and wives) who enjoy being paid for a sociable day in the country.

When I made up my mind to stop at the end of 2010/11 season, Margaret and I hosted a family day. Everybody shooting was a Nelstrop or married to

Joanna with an English partridge which she took out of a covey well in front.

one. The grandchildren and their mothers were out bush beating and the children who stuck it all day got paid. Eliza and her second cousin Emily (aged 10) left the party at lunch to cook something for tea! Lots of photos were taken. One year later George (aged 9) shot his first partridge with his 4.10 – life moves on! Most guests will agree that the hospitality and catering at Westfield is always a highlight – on a bad or wet day it is *the highlight!* We start with a coffee and sausages in the fingers. Margaret has made a lot of sloe, damson, plum gin, etc which is sampled mid-morning. At midday everyone stays outside – no boots off, etc – for bacon and cheese filled baked potatoes, hot grog, Guinness cake and Auntie Jill's. The last drive starts before 3.00 pm. Traditionally Margaret cooked a partridge for each gun and guest, but now we go off to Washingborough Hall for four ribs of beef and all the trimmings.

The family bush beaters on the family day.

Other shoots and memories

I started shooting at a time when wild pheasants and particularly wild English pheasants were abundant. The keeper's job was to control vermin and to feed – very little rearing. The diary records that in 1970 we joined with Tinsleys on our east side on three successive Fridays in September to shoot English partridge. The bags were wonderful (can't find the figures) and we thought it would never end, but it did almost overnight. At the second of these days, brother James brought the motor racing legend Jack Brabham, who farmed in Australia. Jack had never shot game before and, under supervision and being very safety conscious, he didn't do much damage at first, but suddenly he clicked and, with the good eye he undoubtedly had, he was very impressive in the afternoon.

At the same time there was a regular Wednesday shoot at the Longhills Farm – Ted Scoley (a brilliant shot who pointed at the bird and pulled the trigger) farmed Longhills and rented the Co-op farm land. We met at 10.00 am having done the shepherding, had a picnic lunch, and finished before 3.00 pm. Tom Stiff, the retired Nocton keeper, organised it and seemed to only need regular tots of whisky to keep going. As we all left to do our evening sheep and cattle, Ted would say "same time next week."

There were a few characters. Billy Gilliatt, a local tobacconist with a barber's shop had a Purdey gun which had belonged to Joe Kennedy (father of Jack, Bob, Edward, etc) when he was American Ambassador to London. I should like to have bought it, but Billy died and his widow quickly sold it.

Billy and one or two other older statesmen needed watching very carefully – they were safe but we didn't number in those days and they knew where to be. If they were fumbling about near the vehicles – don't rush – but if they set off like a hare it was time to be in front!

One of my favourite days throughout my shooting career was with the Ireland family at Ermine Street, Ancaster. On my first visit after the third drive which went wrong Mr Stan Ireland and the keeper Jack Smith had a blazing row – ok, but they were at opposite corners of a wood. The upshot was that Smith got sacked, but not for the first time (I found out later). He said "I am not going Mr Stan. He never did go and died 'in harness' many years later.

Jack Smith was aided by two assistant keepers who on shoot days before radios and mobile phones were the outside flagmen. There used to be a regular call "ware ar yer Alberrt" followed by "am eer". On at least one occasion one of the shooting guests caused mayhem by calling "am eer" from the wrong side of the wood.

I was very privileged to shoot with the late Roger Fletcher in his early days. He was the best shot I have ever seen. On one occasion at Ram Farm as Chris Howard's guest, we were all in line walking up a field of stubble to our positions, when a covey of English partridge got up at Roger's feet – he shot three with the first shot and one with the second. The covey then turned in the wind and came back over him when he got a left and right – Chris has a different memory but it still adds up to six birds with four shots out of one covey.

One day I went to Morton Fen near Bourne – I was surprised at the instruction – "shoot the hens it is them that lays the eggs". An odd instruction but I soon discovered why – the rough ploughed fen fields were crawling with pheasants – they were vermin! On another occasion at a wood near Skendleby we started by shooting several left and rights at very sleepy woodcock, then realised the wood was *full* of woodcock which had migrated in on a full moon on the previous night. We stopped, pulled out and left.

About 15-20 years ago I had two big numbers days at the end of the season. A couple of hens fell at my feet and we looked at each other for a few moments until they died. I didn't enjoy it and by the time I had got home from the second day I decided not to shoot for a year and think about it. I had a good season, standing with young men to safely shoot their first birds, picking up with my dog, bush beating, etc.

At the end of the season, on the first Saturday in February, (which is National Pigeon Day), I took my gun, shot a couple of pigeons and declared I was back to shooting; no longer did I want to kill because they were there. I much enjoyed several more years being selective and trying to wipe my neighbour's eye.

One of the best bits for me has been the company of my various dogs and our joint efforts at picking up. I am lost without a dog. I have never had a brilliant dog, but have had character dogs. Some could have been very good with a better owner! There is great satisfaction in your dog coming back with a dead bird on a difficult retrieve.

At Otby several years ago my black cocker bitch Sox went missing at the end of the last drive. It was getting dark and coming on to rain. Everybody was ready for home but I said I daren't go home without her and continued to shout and whistle. She must have gone after a runner down a rabbit hole because eventually she arrived as a very scruffy brown cocker.

One of my favourite shoots is Worlaby belonging to the Lamyman family. Just before surgery in 2007 I had finished with chemotherapy and radiotherapy and was beginning to feel a bit better and stronger, Keith Gilbert invited me as his guest. I took Bill Hodgson to carry a few things and prop me up. My friends told me later that with my black balaclava I looked awful *but* it was a wonderful tonic. I shot a few (very few) but Bill kept telling me what a wonderful shot it was and most birds were mine!

On my very last day before stopping shooting at the end of 2010/11 season I had Bill Hodgson with me and everything was magical and memorable. We set off with difficult mainly crossing birds in a quarry and the afternoon was spent at Oxcombe. I 'threw my gun' at all the super high birds and several fell – a super climax to a memorable and happy shooting career.

I fired three cartridges at Westfield during the 2011/12 season and then put my gun away – I couldn't feel the trigger finger *but* I have now had my two carpel tunnel operations and I can feel it again. I wrote my thank you and goodbye letter at the end of 2010/11 season – I think it says it all.

HARVEST COTTAGE
11 CHURCH LANE, COLEBY, LINCOLN LN5 0AQ
TELEPHONE: 01522 810226   FAX: 01522 811668

1 February 2011

All good things must come to an end. After 54 years of very great pleasure, fantastic sport and enjoying the company of great people and friends, I have decided to stop shooting, before someone tells me I should! Or I fall over!

A long list of medical reasons is inappropriate; suffice it to say I am slow and getting slower. I have wonderful memories of shooting, drives and particular memorable shots (mine and others) and events. I have met and enjoyed hosts, keepers, beaters and pickers up; and enjoyed fantastic hospitality.

When the last of my 6 unmarried Nelstrop Aunts died in 1970, Aunt Gertie left me £3000. My Spanish AYA had gone wrong and I took myself to see old Mr Elderkin at Spalding and bought a very nice pair of Charles Ingram side by side 12 bore. I hadn't received my legacy so paid with a company cheque book just filling in the counterfoil 'Game Harvesters', then I forgot all about it, but eight months later my accountant asked what these 'Game Harvesters' were for. Over the years I have found them remarkably accurate IF ONLY I have pointed them in the right direction.

The desire to kill is not so keen and for the last 10 years I have subconsciously tried to shoot good birds and very occasionally my neighbour's bird when he has finished with it. You may remember that I had a year off about 15 years ago and I had a lot of pleasure accompanying young men to shoot their first pheasant, and picking up with my dog.

As a dirty boot yeoman farmer, part of the pleasure is in visiting the same farm every year and observing and enjoying all that is good in farming and the many changes that have taken place, and for many years a busy shooting season in November and December resulted in much thought and planning with action and change in January and February.

For some time I have been counting my blessings regarding life in general, good health, a wonderful wife and great children with lovely daughters in law and grandchildren. Included in these blessings I consider we are very privileged to enjoy our shooting and all that it entails in Lincolnshire England.

3 men and 1 woman stand out in my sporting life and I owe a lot to them, Chuck and Bob Hanson, who between them did 102+ years for the Nelstrop family, taught me as a child and youth and later as their boss much about 'the ways of the countryside', vermin control, pigeon shooting and good farming and rural practice and having a very lame father who had served in the first war and didn't fire a gun except at a crow stealing walnuts. It was them who took me out shooting and got me going. Later it was Bob with his bantams and coups who got the Westfield shoot going, firstly by looking after the English partridge and rearing pheasants and much later adapting to French partridge and maize. Many of my friends will agree that the Westfield shoot is a bit special. Robert and I do it for fun with our friends and have resisted the pressures to go commercial.

The third man is Raymond Shipley who first came to run our days. Bob Hanson was better with game than he was at organising the beaters. Through a process of negotiation with the late Patrick Dean and later his son James, we have evolved to today's shoot, where I invariably do what he suggests! His advice and running of the Westfield shoot has been exceptional and very much appreciated.

The one woman is Margaret, who has organised the job, sent out invitations, written game cards and who has fed and watered many mouths over the years and has become notable for her coffee and sausage starts, damson and sloe gin mid morning, baked potatoes with fillings, 'Auntie Jill's favourite' and Guinness cake at lunch, followed by roast partridge and all that goes with it at the end of the day. She has rescued many 'iffy' days and her catering has been a highlight of Westfield shoots – she is my rock!

We had a very special day at Westfield on 30 December, when we had a family day. 7 guns were either a Nelstrop or married to one. Joanna taking William's number shot her first partridge – an English out of a covey taken so far in front that it dropped at her feet. All grandchildren of self and James were bush beaters, who apart from the 3 year olds and the two 10 year old girl cousins, who had an afternoon making cakes, all stuck at it all day and were paid! All very special and we had a photographer to record the day.

A very special shooting life – I now hope to go picking up as much as possible and to carry a gun as no. 0 or no. 9 at Westfield. Life moves on. I now get a lot of pleasure in watching 3 useful shooting sons and picking up the odd bird with Sox.

Shooting stories

Over 55 years of game shooting there are bound to be a few little stories as well as wonderful memories of special shoots, guns, birds, beaters, keepers, etc. etc.

1. Wansford – When brother James rented the 1,200 acre Cross Leys Farm his farm was part of the Thornhaugh shoot run by Richard Perkins, MD of Perkins Diesel Engines of Peterborough. Thornhaugh Hall was the training centre for the company. James threatened to take the shoot back so a deal was reached for a few years where James had a gun in the shoot. On the day I was invited, I got a puncture on the way, so arrived late and ruffled.

The whole day was very smart and structured and I was highly amused when at the end of the second drive, a Morris 1000 van arrived in a valley clearing in the wood and out got two butlers in formal tails, etc. They produced two card tables, stiff white table cloth, coffee and sausage rolls and they butled! At lunch the same men served us in the splendid dining room.

2. Mervinslaw and Falside – I called to see my neighbour Miles Pole one bitterly cold afternoon whilst staying at Mervinslaw. He produced a bottle of whisky, threw the cork in the fire and as far as I remember we drank it. He invited me to shoot with him the next week, so after a snowy night I turned up with gun. The party laboured all morning through snow laden ten year-old pine trees just high enough for the snow to go down your neck.

At lunch the bag was one cock pheasant, which I had shot. We went into the house for our packed lunch and some 'liquid warmth' and when we came out a dog had eaten the pheasant. We got on slightly better in the afternoon.

3. Royal Command – My good friend Bill Taylor, my bank manager at Peterborough, was the mad keen Secretary of the British Retriever Society who were holding their trials at Sandringham. He invited me to go as a number board carrier – this involved a special shaft on to which I quickly fixed the number of the competitor running their dog in line with the guns and judges and two competitors. This was for the benefit of both judges and spectators who were some way back. The trials were at Wolferton Marsh and Her Majesty was present in the line all day. I thought it was amazing that nobody checked the six guns or me out for security and was highly privileged to be there.

Toward the end of the day the competition was down to the last three dogs and the procedure was changed from walking up to the driven birds. I was aware that many of us were in the way, so did Her Majesty and we received the command "I think we should get in the ditch" – so we did!

4. Grouse shooting – My good friend Ray Ollerenshaw invited me to shoot grouse on his moor above Lady Bower Reservoir where the dam had been used for practice by the Dambusters planes before their famous raid. On the first drive in the loveliest bit of England I was fortunate to shoot two crossing birds in front of me. At the end of the drive a picker-up came and was obviously impressed with this chap from Lincolnshire who could shoot them so far out in front. On this day and three other days at the grouse, I never got another bird!

It is on this moor that Geoff Eyres (Ray's son-in-law) has done a wonderful job of heather regeneration by developing a heather seed harvester and a heather seed drill.

On another occasion in 1976 I was asked to shoot on the Glorious 12th on a tiny but productive moor near Carlisle. One of the guests of Joe Raine, Chairman of the NFU Livestock Committee, was Henry Plumb the President of the NFU, later to become Sir Henry, then Lord Plumb and Chairman of the EU. Son Charles carried his gun, etc. all day. Lord Plumb, aged 85+, spoke brilliantly at the Lincolnshire NFU Annual General Meeting in 2013 and vividly remembered the occasion. This moor, surrounded by the most wonderful productive grassland where you can nearly see the grass growing, was so small that the same ground was done four times – north to south, south to north, east to west, west to east, but there was plenty of grouse.

5. Oops – Several years ago I shot at Welton le Marsh with my old pal Rob Smith and his stepson Jan. We were a jolly party all travelling round together in a gun bus. We went to Firsby for two drives – one at duck and one to do a drive never done before on a bit of new land. We received our instruction that nos. 2-4 would be in one field and 5-8 next door separated by a high hedge with small house adjacent. James Measures, no. 1, asked where he should go and was told 'go where you like James'. 'I shall stand in front of John Grant (no. 4)' he said quietly. I was no. 6, so didn't see all the action but at the start of the drive a very good cock pheasant flew down the hedge line. There was a single shot and a very dead pheasant fell onto and through the conservatory roof. James apparently moved quickly back to where he should have been and let John (Killer) Grant take the blame.

6. Husbands and wives – I attended a gun dog trial on the Brocklesby Estate in North Lincolnshire. Among the guns was Bill Kirkby and his then wife. Bill, the perfect husband and gentleman, carried her gun to the first drive, during which she 'wiped his eye' twice – after which she was noisily told in no uncertain terms that "you can carry your own bloody gun."

7. Hare shooting – Many years ago in my youth, I turned out in a February snow storm to shoot hares at British Crop Dryers. On the first drive crouching behind one of the many fallen down stone walls on the estate, I shot four or five big hares. This very cold hare shooter had to carry them all back to the vehicles over two large fields. I have to confess to 'shooting to miss' after the first two kill for the rest of the day.

8. An early lunch – Two or three years ago I was shooting on a Saturday with the Battle family at Potterhanworth. I knew we were going to the newly-restored Chequers pub for lunch and after a very good partridge drive on the heath, two vehicles led by me paused to speak with Geoffrey, by then suffering from ill health, who had just turned up to join the party for lunch. By the time we got on the road we had lost everybody else so we went to the pub and had just put on shoes when Anthony rushed in the car park to fetch us for another drive. Later in the day I had a wounded bird 200 yards back over an uncrossable water course. Roger Dixon with his one arm had a young dog. It took sometime but I got enormous pleasure from seeing master and dog patiently and persistently working the dog back and then working the hedge line until it retuned with the bird. Memories are made of things like this retrieve and the quiet but obvious elation of the owner and his dog.

9. Safety – Most shooting men know the wonderful poem 'Never, never, let your gun' by Mark Beaufoy, which is full of good advice. We have all tried and mostly succeeded in having a lifetime of care and safety but accidents do happen.

I can remember a few dangerous shots and hairy occasions over the years. There was a regular visitor to Lincolnshire called Ridley from Newcastle who arrived in a Rolls Royce smoking very large cigars and after the first visit was often sent to cover a 'special spot' out of harm's way. I have gone flat on my face occasionally when someone has swing through.

Many years ago I went to a cousin near Retford for a farmers and neighbours day – no beaters – just two lots of guns walking and standing alternate drives. I noticed at the start that there was a selection of guns, hammer guns with the hammers back, stocks strapped up and no sign of gun slings between drives. The last drive of the day was a big wood at Babworth adjacent to the A1 road. I was a member of B gang who were standing with our backs to the A1 whilst the A gang advanced towards us through the wood – I spent the drive behind the biggest tree I could find and didn't bother too much with the pheasants.

I close the safety chapter with an admission of my one lapse which seriously upset me. On a shoot several years ago I pulled my gun out of its sleeve at the start of a drive, broke it to load and there were two cartridges already in. I never could think why but it maybe had something to do with a naughty dog at the end of the previous drive, but no excuse is acceptable.

Getting started again

After writing my letter of retirement at the end of 2010 season and having had carpel tunnel surgery on both hands, I can again feel my trigger finger! So when William told me in 2012 that Rob Brown had asked us to a 'Fathers and Sons' day on his grouse moor in October in Bishopdale off Wensleydale, I accepted with some trepidation, but off we went. I think I wounded a grouse before lunch, but a good job William could hit them. After lunch I missed the first drive whilst recovering from the activities of most of the party getting me over the 4' high fencing and barbed wire fence. I said no way could I get over but with friends and beefy young men on either side lifting legs and giving instructions, I lay along the top of the barbed wire and with much laughing and leg pulling the mission was achieved. Just over the hill 70 yards away was a gateway! At 3.30 pm I thought the day was over but it was announced that we would have a partridge drive off the hill. I took a couple of paracetamol and told William I would shoot – fantastic high and crossing birds. A lucky kill followed by a right and left and suddenly the infirmities and aches of old age were forgotten. I am delighted to report that on a January 2013 day at Westfield with George at no. 7 with his single barrel 410 and supervised by his father and me at no. 0, George shot and picked five French partridges, whilst I got (and was pleased with) two or possibly three.

Fishing and 'the fish'

Having tired of coarse fishing in Westfield pond, I thought it would be good to catch a salmon. The purchase of Mervinslaw in the Borders gave me a perfect opportunity. I swapped my shooting in the Borders for fishing on the Teviot at Fernilea. As a total novice I made my first mistake. I decided to go alone first time and learn the essentials before going public with a friend.

Having visited the tackle shop at Melrose to get kitted out, I spent a week in November flogging a very full river in water up to my thighs. I suspect there were no fish in the river but it could have been me! The ghillie, Whattie Dodds, (whose son Pete was a full back for Scotland) came occasionally to impart his wisdom but didn't inspire me! I spend a lot of time taffled up in the riverside trees and was lucky not to get the hook in my ear. The weather was cold, dull and sometimes windy and it was positively dangerous paddling in waders on the uneven bottom in water 2-3' deep.

My second mistake was to stay alone in the bothy at Mervinslaw – a cold and cheerless place to return to in the dark in November. One day I caught my 'fish'. Suddenly there was something on the line which was going at great speed down river. Excited, I played it for 20 minutes, sometimes winding in, sometimes letting it go, but at all times keeping a tight line. Imagine my delight when with keep net ready I landed a foul hooked stone the shape of a large shoe. 'Bentley's fish' caused a lot of amusement and is still produced for a laugh at my expense.

Later with Sam Wright and Tom Mountain with Margaret in attendance we fished several days at Traquair, near Innerleithen. They caught a fish each and a good time was had by all but it wasn't until the third trip when as a guest of Tom Mountain and David Theaker on the Spey at Grantown (before they bought Mount Hooley) that I at last caught a salmon. Five of us had four ghillies who were very good and got me casting properly and imparted their knowledge of river salmon, water etc. On the last day I got a fish on – it didn't fight much and was easily landed but there it was on the bank a real four or five pound salmon. "Och it's a kelt" said the ghillie and immediately threw it back in the river – not quite what I wanted!

Fishing didn't grab me and I have never fished again, except that I have acted as ghillie to my sons who, as boys, wanted to have a go.

Sheep dog trials

Not a shooting story but a great day out at the National Sheep Dog Trials at Hallrule in the Borders, by invitation of the then Chairman, Ray Ollerenshaw. The invitation included lunch with the officials and guests. After a good morning's competition we gathered for lunch where I was seated next to a wonderful elderly woman – Baroness Elliot. She was the life and soul of the party, dressed in kilt and very stout shoes, cheering everybody with a pint of beer. She told me her late husband Walter Elliot, a brilliant man and MP, had been the Minister of Agriculture when the Milk Marketing Board had been formed, also that he was absent minded and once missed the step at Waverly Station in Edinburgh when alighting from the train and got seriously stuck between the train and the platform and had needed a team of men under the train pushing as well as those above pulling.

Several years later I read a report that she had spoken at a final Milk Marketing Board dinner and got a standing ovation.

As well as being a major landowner, she was a shareholder of Lanark Mart – Laurie & Symington. She told me her big week consisted of a day at Lanark on Monday then she caught the night sleeper to London, she attended the Lords on Tuesday to Friday and assured me she was very busy, but when I saw her in the Lords on TV she always seemed to be asleep! Back home on the Friday night sleeper, she spent Saturday either following hounds or dealing with farming and estate matters, but she was keen to tell me that on Sunday she always played the organ at the Kirk at Bonchester Bridge. At this point the man on the other side of me, Timmy Douglas a well known local worthy whispered to me in a voice many could hear "high on enthusiasm but low on accuracy".

The Rutting Buffalo

In approximately 1993 a lot of good friends were invited by Stuart and Pauline Hemington to stay for a week at Persie Mains House near Bridge of Cally, Perthshire. We had a great week with each family producing the evening meal once.

On one day golfers past and present went to a neighbouring hotel near Glen Shea and played golf on the highest nine-hole course in Scotland. I hadn't played for 28 years, so had taken my old left-handed clubs with hickory shafts. I then discovered that golf had moved on in the 28 years and that my balls were much smaller than all the others!

The first tee was adjacent the hotel car park with the green 50 feet below over the river – wonderfully picturesque and quite challenging. I addressed the ball, swung and the ball got over the river, but into very rough. The photo is of the author threshing about in the long grass – I was likened to a 'rutting buffalo' and the name stuck!

20 years later four or five men, who haven't improved one little bit over 20 years, play annually in Lincolnshire for the 'Rutting Buffalo' trophy, a magnificent wooden buffalo brought from Africa, whilst the ladies of the party play for the 'Old Cow', a not very beautiful blue and white pottery cow.

After our strenuous afternoon, the party go on to Sue and Anthony Battle's for a delicious cold supper and the presentation of the awards! Great fun!

The Rutting Buffalo.

PEOPLE AND FRIENDS

Yesterday's men – sadly dead

Yesterday's men who were exceptional in ability, character and help to me, who influenced me and whose memory I treasure:

1. My father – 46 when I was born was, very quiet and with immaculate judgement, he was my best friend.

2. G. R. Forbes – Headmaster and owner of St Hugh's School, Woodhall Spa. His methods were extraordinary but just after the war there was no money about. Very limited facilities but a very happy school. I can still name the 120 boys on the long photograph – they would nearly all agree with me.

3. Chuck and Bob Hanson – see the chapter on the Hanson family.

4. Eric Morley – A true craftsman and model farm worker. Eric could do everything and is well remembered now for all the tree planting, hedge planting and plashing and estate management.

5. My father-in-law, Jack Fletcher, who gave me his eldest daughter.

6. Lol Bembridge – Pedigree Lincoln cattle breeder par excellence, who proposed our health at our wedding and who did so much for Lincolnshire farming.

7. Philip Stone, our accountant, who gave so much good family advice over the years.

8. Max Howard of Nocton – did a huge amount of work in so many ways for the benefit of agriculture and The Lincs. Agricultural Society.

9. Patrick Dean of Mere – my neighbour – sometimes very naughty but kind, helpful, especially to my children when students with him at Mere. A great shot.

10. Richard Bevan – came to Lincoln as Agricultural Manager at Midland Bank. His background was dairy farming and estate management in the Wirral, much of it for Lord Leverhulme. He was a character and became a great

Eric, Chuck and Bob at the entrance to Westfield Farm. The Centenary Plantation 1981 is on the right.

friend. With no banking expertise, but a great feel for men and business he built up a huge profitable business and was much liked and respected. On retirement he took on several high profile and prestige jobs – Governor at Harper Adams, Chairman of the Parker Group and several Nickerson family businesses.

11. Roger Spurrier – a gentleman Land Agent, straight as an arrow, trusted me and gave me the chance to farm and helped to buy Linwood as well as many other business deals and shooting days out.

12. Billy Parker of Blankney – A self-made man who ended up owning approx. 40,000 acres. He lived at Heacham in Norfolk. A book should have been written about him and his exploits. There are many stories of his bets and the story of how he came to buy the Blankney Estate. His main contribution to Lincolnshire farming was his deep ploughing of the Lincoln heath, which together with the combine drill turned a large area from sheep and rabbits to some of the best arable farm land.

13. Henry Dickinson – His ashes are spread at Canwick Manor Farm, where he found joy and job satisfaction having escaped from the Scunthorpe Steel works. He went on to become Foreman.

14. Tom Horstwood – I inherited Tom when I rented the Poplars at Linwood. He was totally competent, loyal and dependable.

The Centenary Wood 32 years later with Molly and Sox.

List of exceptional men and women – living

There is a second list of exceptional men who are still alive, whom I must mention:

1. My brother James – enough elsewhere in the book.

2. Dick High – a brilliant ADAS Advisor until illness struck him down. In his MGBGT he influenced my farming decisions for years.

3. Andrew Wylde – long serving family solicitor. A little time to think things out – then wonderful sound adviser – unlike many of today's solicitors he could handle every problem and situation.

4. Chris Howard – perhaps unfair to single out Chris from my local friends and other partners in the Co-operative. Always the prime mover with the purchase of Spaldings from Spalding and Son, Branston Engineering and selling to Hungary etc, but particularly his drive and leadership of Branston Potatoes, which has made our family a lot of money!

5. Geoffrey Taylor – Tax and Financial Advisor, Streets. Geoff planned and orchestrated the family de-merger in 1999. He got Inland Revenue consent to split a Limited Company. The family did exactly as advised and came out the other end as four independent businesses with everybody happy and no tax paid!

6. Tony Meggitt – long suffering and loyal farm worker and family friend. Started aged 14 and apart from 2-3 years when the family emigrated to Australia, has worked for various family members including being Foreman

for a time. Has many stories to tell of exploits all over Lincolnshire with peas, contracting, etc. Also very involved with Margaret as the person who did all sorts of jobs for her and the boys, including school runs and rescuing 'motoring misfortunes'.

7. Richard Harris of Potato & Allied Services and McCain – an enthusiastic and technically brilliant knowledge of potato storage, sprout and suppressants. Later a huge influence in the world of processed potatoes and latterly Mr Political Potato on committees in Brussels.

8. Paul Clarke of Nocton – he and Anne brought daffodils to Nocton in a big way – with up to 600 eastern European casuals, investment and direct marketing to Marks & Spencer and all over Europe.

9. Dr Eremin, Mr Suresh Pillai, my surgeon, and all at Lincoln County Hospital Intensive Care and Oncology Department whose professional care and expertise mean that I am still alive to write this book.

10. Hugh and Marion Mair – Great friends to Margaret at Blankney Fen before I came on the scene. They share our Wedding Anniversary, but are seven years in front of us. We meet up every year on our Anniversary for a nice lunch and to swap gossip.

11. Our neighbours – Thank you for your friendship and occasional help.

My best friend, Michael

In approximately 1944 the Scoley family came to live next door at St John's farm. Michael is a little older but we have been very involved with each other ever since. We were in the same set at St Hugh's School and I remember getting the winning 'gold' which meant that Michael as captain of 'blue set' got his name on the shell case.

Michael's mother Dorothy was very ill for a period in 1947 and he spent the summer holiday with us and he went with us to Llandudno for a family holiday.

When he married Jill in 1961 at Coleby, where we now live, I was very privileged to be his best man and also to be godfather to Meryl. Our paths have been remarkable

RBN and Michael at Llandudno...

...also with Ted Scoley and the Wolseley.

together for our married lives, children and parties, Branston Co-op, farming neighbours and more recently as 'paid' up members of the Pottergate Golf Club where we play rutting buffalo type golf on a Wednesday afternoon. We have had lessons but are rather worse than we were 15 years ago.

Our great enjoyment is the company, the exercise and laughing at each others misfortunes with a little white ball – we get a lot of laughs.

Lady Miriam Rothschild of Ashton Manor, near Oundle

Out of the blue 10 or 15 years ago I received an invitation from Mrs Miriam Lane to attend an open day at Ashton Manor – lunch would be provided! I was intrigued – who was Miriam Lane and why me? Much investigation revealed that Miriam Lane was Lady Miriam's married name and that she was (in an eccentric way) miles 'ahead of the field' in providing habitats for birds, bees, butterflies, insects, fleas etc on her large estate at Ashton Wold.

I fortunately replied that Margaret and I would be delighted to attend. I found out that the late Lol Bembridge was also invited, so off we went.

At Ashton we turned off the highway next to the pub where the World Conker Championships are held annually and the long track kept getting narrower, bumpier and more overgrown until we arrived together with several others in a clearing with a large totally overgrown house including vegetation over the windows and roof. Lady Miriam was the world expert on butterflies and moths and the house housed the best reference library in the world with laboratories and meeting rooms – what a surprise! We were taken to see clover leys and wild flower mixes alive with wildlife, tumble down wonderful old buildings with a story to tell and a large area of the 2nd World War airfield at Polebrook, which was being managed for wildlife. We then returned for a splendid lunch with magnificent Rothschild wines and a talk from the wheelchair-bound hostess – Lady Miriam. It was her custom to entertain conservationists annually but this year she had decided to have practical working farmers with an interest in conservation, both to see what she was doing and to keep her up to speed with farming and food production.

After lunch we were invited to explore the garden – there was a mown area about 20' x 20' for Lady Miriam to have tea with her grandchildren. The rest was a magnificent wilderness with two or three paths kept for access.

Lady Miriam told me "I have only got one gardener you know!" I quietly wondered what on earth he did!

As we left, the library was again in use by visiting scientists and the dining room was being prepared for dinner with all the best silver, glass and cutlery, presumably for Lady Miriam to entertain visiting naturalists.

A very special day out – Lady Miriam is long dead, but there is a roundabout outside Oundle which she planted up with wild flowers – what a woman!

Students

For years we had a student each year – usually a middle year in a three year college course. Additionally we collected up some summer students to do the pea vining harvest.

From a list of thirty males and one female (Sarah Barker), I shall mention just a few who for various reasons left their mark.

Neil Westcott came for a pea season – an ambitious young farmer who lived with us – a brilliant pianist, singer and composer – now farms half of Australia near Parkes.

Henry King – a very clever academic had (like his brother) been Head Boy at Winchester, but not terribly practical. He arrived for work on day one with a long mackintosh, gym shoes and no hat – Margaret took him in hand.

John Alvis and Geoffrey Wright – great lads and highly competent. John farms 100's of cows producing cheddar cheese for the family business in Cheshire and Geoffrey works in the city but has a farm to come home to one day.

John Morrow – full of enthusiasm and talk but often a figure of ridicule. He was always going to show the farm men how to do it better and faster – he never did and there are fond memories of him 'throwing' his beet gapping hoe down and leaving in floods of tears.

Stephen Betts – not strictly a student – a very nice young man who had been incarcerated at the Bracebridge Heath Mental Hospital because he had very bad fits. We were asked if we would have him to work part time, not easy to find a job on a farm, but over several years he was kindly looked after by the farm men especially Bob. His medication improved his condition and he later moved on getting a good job at RAF Cranwell, buying his own house and getting a driving licence – a success story.

Ben Hardy – a very impressive young man training to be a vet and now in academic life at Cambridge. He went to work for David at Linwood and was a bit accident prone. In harvest time he was carting grain from combine to store. The procedure in store was to back up to a very old, heavy and long Wytrac elevator with a 12" swinging end. After tipping each trailer a chain was attached to the tractor to pull the elevator forward 6" ready for the next load. Ben omitted to take the chain off. He set off back to the field with his empty trailer with elevator in tow. How he got out the shed without hitting something nobody knows. He travelled 100 yards down the farm entrance road, halted at the Market Rasen-Wragby road B1202, then turned right and set off flat out in top gear. After about 300 yards there is a dip and whilst going downhill the chain came off and the elevator now a 25 mph missile careered across the road and came to rest over a small ditch and embedded in a hedge. The elevator being built like a battleship was undamaged, nobody coming the other way was injured and all that was needed was a new electric cable.

James Arden – James came aged 16 as a YOP (Youth Opportunities Person). 25 years later he recently left to pursue a new career as an electrician. Self-taught in all aspects of arable agriculture, sprayer operations, potato planting and harvesting, beet harvester driver, mechanic, stone wall builder, etc. – a great fellow.

James Leethem Nelstrop – The English Whisky Co., St George's Distillery

James was born in 1945 when our parents were 53 and 33. Father was extremely lame and James was as much brought up by the men on the farm, especially the Hanson family who taught him the ways of the country, fishing, ferreting, etc. He was sent to St Hugh's Prep School and Worksop College and on leaving aged 16 he found that I, aged 23, was fully in charge at Westfield.

After working on a neighbours farm and studying at Caythorpe Farm Institute, he got a job, aged 20, managing Waddingham Grange Farm for the later Frank Arden who had taken over his father-in-law's farm. Frank thought James was much older! James daren't tell him his real age so he nearly missed his 21st party when Frank wanted him elsewhere. In quick succession James resigned in 1968, came to live at Canwick Manor Farm, advertised for and bought Cross Leys Farm Wansford, 1,200 acres, which was sold on to the Church Commissioners on a lease-back arrangement. They built a new farmhouse and huge shed including 1000 tonne insulated potato store. In 1974 James became disenchanted with being a tenant, split the partnership with me and sold his 50% share in Canwick Manor Farm and went off to farm in Australia, buying Kaloola near Dubbo in New South Wales, 2000 acres, with a new air-conditioned house which he bought outright.

After nearly two years farming wheat and sheep a few things conspired to make him sell up. Barbara was homesick, James had a bad back and

James on a pony.

sitting on a tractor was a pain. Also, despite having two good harvests James had studied the weather records and realised he was in a drought area. Someone came along and offered a good price so he sold and came to England – officially on holiday before the next project but he never went back.

He then purchased Roudham Farm, 700 acres, near Thetford, very dry and sandy but plenty of irrigation water for potatoes, onions, etc. as well as 100 acres of asparagus. Having built this into a very successful business and added

James' 21st party at Westfield, which he very nearly missed.

a garden centre, he sold out to Tim Jolly and family and came and bought Blyborough Grange Farm near Kirton Lindsey, 1500 acre, houses, good dryer and a let-out piggery. This had been farmed rather badly by a big farming company as contractor to the Post Office Pension fund. This was a good farm farmed by a young Andrew Nelstrop which for several years produced good crops, *but* Andrew has a serious allergy to gluten and he had to keep out the way of combine, drier, grain stores and the piggery – very unsatisfactory so they sold out to a man who had sold a car business for multi-millions.

James' and Barbara's wedding day.

Andrew went home to Norfolk and whilst James bought a worn out blackland farm on the border of Norfolk and Suffolk and put it all down to environmental schemes, Andrew tried his hand at building.

There followed several years of house building and developing sites as well as converting all the farm buildings to houses for personnel from the American airbase at Lakenheath. James saw the 'writing on the wall' for the overheated house building industry two years before it happened and slowed down. Then

Andrew, Lizzie, James and Barbara.

James had the great idea to produce whisky. Our father had often questioned why the whisky had to be made in Scotland when the best malting barley was in eastern England. James just happened to have a site at Roudham near East Harling with two good boreholes, good road access and a picturesque setting with the river Thet as a boundary. Early samples of the water were encouraging, the authorities generally were in favour but the planners initially wanted the distillery on an industrial estate – not ideal. Permission was granted, the house building team were transferred to build the distillery, James employed a well-known master whisky producer, called Ian Henderson, who just happened to have retired to live with his daughter at Swaffham and he organised the Scottish equipment manufacturer of distillery equipment, including all the copper equipment, etc.

There followed three years of production of spirit into bourbon barrels to produce single malt at three years old. During which time bonded warehouses, shop and teaching rooms were finalised together with several concoctions including Norfolk Nog, a 'Baileys' type creamy drink but much more powerful and an established favourite on a Norfolk shooting day.

A potential problem is that as the only producer of English Whisky there is nobody with whom to blend, etc. This is offset by producing some batches peated and some smoked.

HRH Prince Charles at the Official Opening of St George's Distillery, March 2007.

The Whisky Distillery at Roudham.

The water from the in-house bore is of the very highest quality coming from the chalk under Breckland and consequently makes a very fine spirit.

James and Andrew are also entrepreneurial in the procurement and use of used bourbon and sherry barrels, together with packaging and marketing of a very fine product.

Brother James – a few problems

A few days after Margaret and I got engaged in 1962, Father went off to see his tenant Dick Pick at Canwick Manor Farm. They did a deal and for £2,000 Dick relinquished his tenancy. This bought him a new three bed bungalow at Bracebridge Heath, somewhat ironically in Bentley Drive.

Whilst the farmhouse was empty we did a few jobs before moving in, including laying on mains water and removing the old water system of windmill and holding tanks in the barn roof. The windmill was over the well which was unfortunately just outside the kitchen window so that the nice southerly view was obliterated by windmill steel going in every direction.

The day appointed for removing the windmill did not go well. We should have had more sense! We decided that with a long rope attached to a tractor we could cut off all four legs at ground level and pull the steel pyramid over the centre of balance and that it would fall in the available space.

James on the tractor was instructed to go quite quickly but he selected a low gear resulting in the rope going slack, and the windmill twisted and settled comfortably on the sitting room roof! After a brotherly fall out and much swearing and abuse, it was decided to keep going and pull it off! 30 years later a telescopic fork lift truck would have quickly sorted it out but we had nothing but ropes. The upshot was we got the windmill down, cut up and removed but serious repairs were needed to the roof and the corner of the wall.

Whilst James was home for six months before taking the Wansford farm, he had a project concreting the road from Canwick Manor to the bungalow on the corner of Canwick Avenue, a distance of approx 900 yards x 9' wide. He got well organised and he and Eric did 2 or 3 ready mix loads a day. It wasn't until 700 yards down with 200 to go that he discovered that his measuring stick for setting up the shuttering was 8' wide only! Many years later we added another 2'.

Perhaps someone else invented them but in the 1960s James designed and built the very first lamb adopter. It was a brilliant bit of kit at lambing time with a difficult ewe and orphan lamb. He made quite a lot and all the local sheep farms had one or more. There are now lots of various models available – I think James' was the first.

108   *The proceedings and accounts.*   [... June

[1608] Richard Wyffin.	Iohn Bouth.
Robert Barnes.	William Burket.
George Hill. (26)	Nicholas Ven.
George Pretty.	William Perce.
Iohn Taverner.	Francis Perkins.
Robert Cutler.	Francis Perkins.
Michaell Sieckelmore.	William Bentley.
Thomas Coo.	Richard Gradon.
Peter Pory.	Rowland Nelstrop.
Richard Killingbeck.	Richard Salvage.
William Causey.	Thomas Salvage.
Doctor Russell.	Gent. Richard Myler.
Richard Worley.	William May.
Richard Prodger.	Vere.
William Bayley.	Michaell.
Richard Molynex.	Bishop Wyles.
Richard Pots.	
Iefry Abots.	Iohn Powell.
Iohn Harper.	Thomas Hope.
Timothy Leds.	William Beckwith.
Edward Gurganay.	William Yonge.
George Forest.	Laurence ...
Iohn Nickles.	William Ward.
William Gryvill.	
	Christopher Rodes.
	Iames Walkings.
Daniel Stalling, Iueller.	Richard Fetherstone.
William Dawson, Refiner.	Iames Burne. 28|
Abraham Ransacke, Refiner.	
William Iohnson, Goldsmith.	Thomas Feld. } Apothecarie
Peter Keffer, a Gunner.	Iohn Harford. }
Robert Alberton, a Perfumer.	Post Gittnat, a C[h]irjurgion
Richard Belfield, Goldsmith.	Iohn Lewes, a Couper.
27|	Robert Cotten, a Tobaco-pipe
Ramon Goodyson.	maker.
Iohn Spearman.	Richard Dole, a black
William Spence.	Smith
Richard Bristow.	and divers others, to the
William Simons,	number of 120.

Labourers (bracketed beside Ramon Goodyson... William Simons)

Pilgrim Fathers – list of those sailing on the 'Phoenix' including Roland Nelstrop.

Paul and Anne Clarke and the daffodils

Paul and Anne sold out of their original Winchester Growers and looked to starting again. They arrived at Nocton (approximately 6,000 acres) in 1990 and set to to farm it very well. They had a lock out from selling daffodils as part of their Winchester sale deal, but that didn't stop them planting a large area of daffodils, which are a two year crop ready for when they could sell again.

Packing sheds, refrigerated stores, grading line etc were installed and in a matter of years Paul had cleaned up the daffodil industry growing 600 acres in Cornwall and 1,000 acres in Lincolnshire. Up to 600 Eastern Europeans were employed, picking and on the packing lines. He installed many static caravans in Cornwall and Lincolnshire and later built a massive hostel block together with swimming pool, sports and health centre, etc for the more permanent staff. He annually supplied M & S with over 20 million bunches as well as exporting around the world. Tulips, lilies, sweet williams and gladioli were also grown and he did a pre-Christmas run of three hyacinths in a terracotta pot covered with moss. The amazing thing to me was the small amount of management used for this enormous business.

Paul the boss and salesman, Anne in the office (imagine paying 600 casuals once a week!), David Longmate in charge of all site activities, Alistair farm and field activities and Robert in charge of all activities in Cornwall.

And then seemingly in the flash of an eye they were sold up and gone – gone back to Wiltshire/Berkshire border where they bought and paid for an 1800 acre estate plus two other 700 acre nearby farms. A more relaxing lifestyle back in the area of their youth with old friends – how very sensible.

For several years I let 40 or 50 acres for daffodils, sometimes picked for flowers, sometimes for bulbs – We miss the colour in March and April and the friendship of Paul and Anne.

Webbed Feate

When we got engaged, Margo's mother and father had a party for their friends and to meet the future son-in-law. Edgar Gilbert, who spoke Lincolnshire loudly and with great humour, on meeting me said,

"Did ya nua yar intendeds got webbed feate she is a fen gel."

I haven't found them yet!

Roland Nelstrop

There is evidence that this Quaker gentleman sailed to the New World with the Pilgrim Fathers in 1608. Nothing is known of him – could there be a family branch in America?

George Tokarski and Margaret

Many readers will remember the photographer's shop in Lincoln High Street. George fled Poland when the Russians advanced towards Germany early in the war, got to England and joined the Polish section of the Royal Air Force.

He met Mother's sister Margaret when he was stationed at RAF Dunholme Lodge flying 35 missions in Wellington Bombers from RAF Hemswell in bomber raids over Germany. I have his flight book. George was navigator and wireless operator and it wasn't until he died and a medal was found in a drawer which nobody knew about, including his wife Margaret, that it was discovered that it was the 'Cross of Valour' with 3 bars – *Virtuti Militari* – the Polish equivalent of the Victoria Cross awarded for bringing home a bomber and its crew with a dead pilot.

The Polish community knew about this and the medal was carried on a purple cushion at his funeral. I could never understand why George was so committed to fighting the Germans in the war when it was the Russians who murdered his father and destroyed Krakow and much of Poland in their advance on Germany.

After the war George pursued his interest in photography after recovering from TB where he was hospitalised at Midhurst for a long period. He and Margaret started with an 'at home business' with a dark room in the outbuildings at Welton before renting the shop in the High Street which they subsequently bought.

Devout Roman Catholics, they never missed church on Sunday and did a huge amount for the church and charities, especially the Leonard Cheshire VC and Sue Ryder Homes.

For many years they sent food parcels and essentials to George's widowed mother in Krakow before Communism finally relented and let her come to live out her days in England. George was a gentleman with strong Christian ethics.

OTHER

UFO in the bottom grass field

One morning around 1965, Bob arrived for work at 7.00 am in a very excited state. From the seat of his bicycle he had glimpsed a large bright something over the hedge in a very wet little four-acre permanent grass field. Two of them went off to intercept the aliens and found an abandoned bus. Someone during the night had stolen a single decker bus and for some reason best known to them had driven the bus into the grass field and had got it well stuck. The site of this alien landing is now part of the eight million gallon reservoir.

Hedges and trees

I make no apology for having pulled out miles of hedges and quite a lot of trees.

The man who planted the hedges on Westfield at the time of the enclosures was probably permanently drunk – there isn't a straight hedge on the farm.

Having removed useless hedges to make sensible sized fields, we have over the years planted new hedges, many trees both in hedge rows and plantations on all the farmed land usually without a grant.

I have made several mistakes – if only the hedges planted were just blackthorn or hawthorn instead of an unlikely mixture containing hazel, rose and several other species.

In 1981 to celebrate 100 years as tenants at Westfield we planted a triangular plantation at the road end and Margaret has planted 'Hansons Wood' on her small block of land east of Branston.

In 1987 I got into proper trouble when, having bought Longhills Farm, I removed approx 3 acres of useless woodland and snowberry without permission – I never thought about it. A man with a JCB built three or four large heaps ready for burning. I was reported and received a visit from a dark-suited man in a black car with an official-looking black briefcase, who had driven up from London to caution and interview me. He wrote down verbatim everything I said. He visited the scene of the crime (he got his highly-polished black shoes a bit dusty) and measured trunks and quality of timber. On the way I showed him the trees and hedges and conservation work we had done, but it didn't seem to cut any ice. Fortunately when he left me he went to visit Dick High at ADAS Sleaford who put in a good word. At the time I was founder Chairman of Lincolnshire FWAG (Farming and Wildlife Advisory Group) and had visions of the headlines in the *News of the World* – I very quickly resigned! Several weeks later I received a very official looking letter – slapping my wrist – phew!

Banks, lawyers and accountants

I, and the company have been well served. It is all to do with people – not their companies.

Starting with lawyers, I, and the family have been wonderfully fortunate to have Andrew Wylde as family lawyer for as long as I can remember. He retired finally in March 2013. The current trend is for solicitors to specialise, so it is easy to have four or five in the same practice dealing with one's affairs – Andrew did everything – well. We are unlikely to find another!

We as a family have always used Streets as accountants and have had a succession of excellent men. It is not too difficult to add up figures to do profit and loss accounts, but more difficult to give good family advice, pay minimum legal tax and deal with all matters of self-assessment, tax returns, P11D, family trusts, etc.

As a family we were wonderfully advised by Geoff Taylor on demerger in 1997 when, with Inland Revenue approval, we split Nelstrop Farms Ltd into four companies for perfect succession without capital taxation.

The banks are a bit different – I am appalled by their track record of the last few years, but on an individual level and their involvement with agriculture and small family business, we have been well served.

The author and his four sons, 1997; the date we split up the family business.

Father and Grandfather before him had banked with the National Provincial (now NatWest). Father told me in 1956 that he did not know his bank manager and had never borrowed money!

In 1965 when James and I went to borrow money to take on 1200 acre tenanted farm at Wansford, the manager was 'plain stupid' and lost our business. James met Bill Taylor, manager of Midland Peterborough at the East of England Show and we had several very happy years banking with the Midland (now HSBC).

In 1975 brother James had returned to England from Australia and wanted to buy a farm. Midland and most people he approached would not 'play ball' but Wilson Millington at Lloyds Lincoln said he would provide finance for James if I, who by this time was 100% independent from James, would transfer my banking also. I declined to guarantee my brother – the whole arrangement was agreed on trust by a gentleman's handshake. I have always appreciated this, together with Lloyds understanding when in 1985 I made an appointment to tell my manager that I was in 'trouble'. It helped that I knew before they did and I was lucky that my plans including some building plot sales got me out of trouble.

The Church Commissioners as prudent landlords

As far as we can ascertain the Church bought Westfield from Ian Franklin around 1860. He was followed by Robert Giles and James Cartright who died aged 46 in June 1881 and is buried in Kirkstead churchyard.

The Nelstrop family have been there since autumn 1881 when Grandfather Robert moved as a bachelor from Ackworth in Yorkshire. Nothing much changed for 50 years, but the two wars changed everything. For a time the Commissioners were happy to finance improvements, charging 12% on the cost added to the rent. On the face of it, sounds expensive but every three years at the rent review it got lost in the new rent. I worked on the basis that the rent would go up whether or not we had improved. The visit of Church Commissioner approximately every four years, together with officials from Millbank, was a very important event. The agent at Smiths Gore was also treated with great respect. Most visiting Commissioners in the early days had a bit of a quirk, from the man with his enthusiasm for black-leaded grates and red brick floors to the man who was only interested in the gutters which needed cleaning to the tree hugger who was horrified that I wanted to chop down a sycamore tree in the farmyard. It is still there!

They have had a few incentives to improve on conservation matters, such as the specimen trees, which they provided and paid the tenant £25 to plant and look after them. I did a quick calculation and asked for 1000 trees to plant up paddocks and strategic areas – sadly the scheme was for a maximum of 10! The row of very productive walnuts in the front paddock is the result of this initiative.

In the 1980s, without comment, consultation or advice, all of the tenant farms were supplied with an owl box to place in a 'cart shed or equivalent'. The cart sheds or equivalent had all fallen down or been knocked down to make room for modern stores. We installed the box in the roof of the wonderful old pigeon cote and forgot it – nothing happened until the year (1990) when we entered and won the Lincs Agricultural Society Farming and Conservation Awards. I showed the building and the owl box to the judges. One of the judges – Pat Holland of Newball near Langworth – asked if we had any barn owls – I replied "sadly no". "Well" replied Pat "it is upside down." "If you were to turn it the other way up and provide a landing platform in front you may have more success." The next year a barn owl brought off 2 chicks and we have had many families in the pigeon cote since.

Getting back to the Commissioners – in the good old days of landlord and respectful tenant, it was the custom to have a formal dinner at the end of the Commissioners once every four year visit. 'The tenants' were proposed by A Commissioner and the reply was by a senior tenant. My father did the job aged 65 just before I became a tenant and for some reason I was privileged to be asked twice. Once around 1981 when Nelstrops celebrated 100 years at Westfield and again in 1993 at the last dinner before the Church Commissioners had their financial crisis and all such activities stopped. This was at a time when farming was not very profitable – land values and rents were stagnant with some rents coming down. I had farmed the Blankney Fen Farm

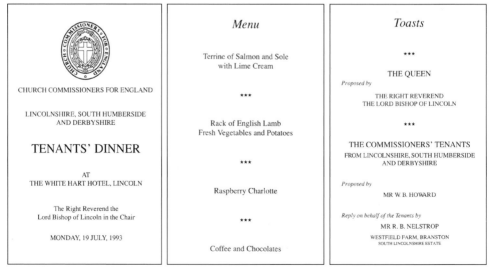

The Last Supper – Lincolnshire Tenants final dinner.

500 acres for a year until a buyer could be found. We were offered it at approximately £1,600/acre with good house, three cottages, etc. I asked my sons who all said no for very good reasons. I remember at the dinner castigating the Commissioners for their policies over English land and for 'selling the family silver'. I was told latter that my remarks had got back to Millbank.

For many years the policy was to build general purpose buildings, with the benefit of hindsight these were all too low for today's equipment and many of the 1960-70s buildings have corroded and need replacing. I wanted an insulated bulk potato store for 550 tonnes in Westfield yard to stand where we had demolished all the old crew yards. The Commissioners were finally persuaded to pay for the 15' high general purpose store with me paying for sleeper walls, insulation of roof and walls, tunnel and fans, doors, etc. It is still a wonderful store having been upgraded by Robert for 600 tonnes refrigerated box storage.

It is interesting to note that the Church Commissioners for England nearly encircle the city of Lincoln with land from the Wragby road roundabout through Greetwell, Washingborough, Canwick, Bracebridge Heath and South Hykeham. They are much involved with the bypass and subsequent development.

In summary, I have been honoured to be a third generation tenant, with Robert the fourth and George and his heirs hoping to continue for many years.

At a time of hardship when the Commissioners were selling farms to their Tenants we were offered Westfield. I wrote to my four sons asking them what they wanted to do. Bearing in mind that they all wanted to farm, the answer was that if we had the cash we would be better to buy another farm!

Church Commissioners and the cat

In approximately 1974 we had a landlord's visit. Our four young sons were drilled to shake hands, call everybody 'Sir' and behave. After the farm inspection, the party was invited to have afternoon tea with cucumber sandwiches in the sitting room! The boys did their stuff and charmed everybody and Margaret brought in tea and sandwiches. To her horror since the morning clean the cat had been in and left a huge deposit. Thinking quickly she picked up the nearby standard lamp and put it on top of the heap.

Energy from renewable sources

The ramblings of an elderly sceptic! A wonderful idea – but!

Much has been said, written and done in the last few years. The sun, water and wave and wind are the most obvious sources and man's ingenuity in harnessing this is amazing. *But* some of us older farmers are horrified at some of the activities involving good agricultural land in the pursuit of biodiesel, electricity and other energies and power sources, both in this county and abroad, particularly maize in the USA and sugar cane in Brazil.

Money comes into the equation from the beginning and all these schemes are heavily subsidised – feed in tariffs, biodiesel subsidy, etc, etc all in the pursuit of Government policy to have 10% of energy from renewable green sources.

Don't get me wrong, we are wasteful and careless with our heritage and much of what is happening is good. AD (anaerobic digester) plants using up waste potato and vegetable products must be right, but if they need 1000's of acres of maize to make them work – not so good. The willow project appears to work well with villages and schools being heated with chopped willow and miscanthus a 20 year crop on third quality land which needs no inputs and ticks a lot of boxes.

I am not sure about the fleet of lorries carting chicken manure to Thetford in Norfolk to fire a power station, but at least the excellent fertilizer 'Fibrophos' comes back to Lincolnshire to grow good crops.

And then there are the wind turbines – I don't dislike them and agree with most that they are better in the North Sea, but they are useless in terms of regular power. No wind – no power. I am sure they will not stand the test of time and then capital and maintenance costs will produce very expensive electricity.

I am in favour of a barrage across the Wash, the river Severn and other obvious places. The bird watchers and naturalists need telling what is going to happen. After a few years all will be back to normal and probably better for wildlife and birds. Costing a lot of money and providing a lot of jobs this at a stroke would harness the sea and produce serious amounts of electricity.

I have never understood carbon footprint, emissions and ozone layers, but was horrified to find that carbon footprints is a tradable commodity between the haves and have nots.

For my part in rural Lincolnshire perhaps I am just about carbon neutral – I have planted a lot of trees and hedges and make good compost in the garden! Margaret and I do our bit with recyclable rubbish – should you use valuable water to rinse a tin before it goes in the green bin or put it in dirty?

FINAL THOUGHTS

Luck is what happens when preparation meets opportunity.

If it ain't broke – don't fix it.

Hold hard.

Get on.

Wayte a minit.

I don't boil my cabbages twice for donkeys.

There are no prizes for martyrs.

Muck and mystery.

Farming matters – well it does to me.

St John 13 v 34

A new commandment I give unto you.
That you love one another as I have loved you.

A farmer's gravestone

Found in the churchyard at Caenby when looking at a farm for sale.

"I thank thee Lord for all thou gave me.
This lovely land, this life, thy light and thy dear love.
For all the Blessings of this wondrous World.
But most of all I thank thee Lord for love."

Lewis Thomas Green, 1902-1986

Seen in a book when I was at Caythorpe College

"I reckon if we have left the land in better order
than we found it we haven't done so bad."

I told you so

With the benefit of hindsight this is very easy to say but not very helpful!

My father never said it to me (he presumably wanted to many times) on the basis that if I was right that was good, but if I was wrong and his advice was right then I probably didn't need telling – I would remember.

As my four sons grew up I resolved never to say 'I told you so' and never did – I hope they carry on the family tradition with their children.

The years have gone

The years have gone I know not where
Lost as by magic in the midst of time
Sorrow in mix with laughter love and joy
The stuff of life that strips the years away
Business and farming, shooting, children, schools
England and Scotland limestone sand and Wold
Have known your touch, the gentle touch of art
This art with science blended in the man
A feel for land, gift of the living God
Bestowed on few – the envy of us all
Respect and admiration both are yours
Live on, live on you still have much to give
Look up with joy look up laugh and live

*Written for a charity booklet by
a Lincolnshire farmer about his North Lincolnshire friend.*

We are survivors

(For those born before 1940…)

We were born before television, before penicillin, polo shirts, frozen foods, Xerox, contact lenses, videos and the pill. We were before radar, credit cards, split atoms, laser beams and ballpoint pens, before dishwashers, tumble driers, electric blankets, air conditioners, drip-dry clothes … and before man walked on the moon.

We got married first and then lived together (how quaint can you be?). We thought 'fast food' was what you ate in Lent, A 'Big Mac' was an oversized raincoat and 'crumpet' we had for tea. We existed before house husbands, computer dating and 'sheltered accommodation' was where you waited for a bus.

We were before day care centres, group homes and disposable nappies. We never heard of FM radio, tape decks, artificial hearts, word processors or young men wearing earrings. For us 'time sharing' meant togetherness, a 'chip' was a piece of wood or fried potato, 'hardware' meant nuts and bolts and 'software' wasn't a word.

Before 1940 'Made in Japan' meant junk, the term 'making out' referred to how you did in your exams, 'stud' was something that fastened a collar to a shirt and 'going all the way' meant staying on the double-decker bus to the terminus. In our day, cigarette smoking was 'fashionable', 'grass' was mown, 'coke' was kept in the coalhouse, a 'joint' was a piece of meat you ate on Sundays and 'pot' was something you cooked in. 'Rock Music' was a fond mother's lullaby, 'Eldorado' was an ice-cream, a gay person was the life and soul of the party, while 'aids' just meant beauty treatment or help for someone in trouble.

We, who were born before 1940, must be a hardy bunch when you think of the way in which the world has changed and the adjustments we have had to make. No wonder there is a generation gap today.

But ... by the grace of God ... we have survived.

The final chapter – our Golden Wedding

Margo and I were married at Blankney Church (where her father was churchwarden) on Saturday 29th June 1963. Margaret has kept everything she could, including details of her wedding dress, photo album, telegrams, notes of costs, wedding service, wedding guests and 131 presents received.

The bride's dress (very beautiful) cost £19, bridesmaid dresses £16 and the reception by Terry's of York (forerunner to Gilpins) including marquee, staff, food and drink was well under £2.50 per head. Of the parents' friends, only Hazel Leach of Blankney is still alive.

Margo and I went to Morning Prayer on Sunday 29th June 2003 to celebrate our Ruby wedding. When we arrived the lovely bells were being rung and I resolved soon afterwards to go back to Blankney for our Golden Wedding, if we both survived!

INVITATION

Limited *Edition*

VINTAGE 1963

BENTLEY AND MARGARET
50TH ANNIVERSARY

50% | A PREMIUM PRODUCT SELECTED AND BLENDED IN THE BRANSTON/ COLEBY REGION | **1963**

VINTAGE 1963

An inspired mix of two varieties gives an elegant blend of wisdom and tolerance mixed with love and laughter. Will keep for many more years but can be enjoyed now with family and friends.

Please join Bentley and Margaret in celebrating their marriage reaching maturity
on Sunday, June 30th. 10.30 a.m. St. Oswalds Church, Blankney, followed by lunch 12.30 p.m Washingborough Hall Hotel

RSVP: HARVEST COTTAGE, COLEBY, 01522810226,
BY JUNE 15TH

I organised for there to be a Prayer Book Communion service on Sunday 30th June and for the bellringers to ring. Invitations were sent out to family and friends for 10.30 am and on a lovely sunny and warm day the party enjoyed the bells for half an hour before entering church. The flowers, beautifully done

for us, were spectacular and we all were uplifted by four favourite hymns, Eliza and brother James reading the set lessons and the sermon being given by our good friend Bishop Bob Hardy, previously Bishop of Lincoln. The local vicar the Rev'd Alan Greenhaugh presided. The organist Judith Rogerson played beautifully, including a very jolly medley after the service including the *The Wedding March*, *The Lincolnshire Poacher* and *Land of Hope and Glory*.

Bishop Bob concluded with the Episcopal Blessing.

We all left church to blazing sunshine, the young grandchildren were waiting to pounce on us with flower petals just outside the lychgate and we found the Bentley with hood down and gold lamé wedding ribbons, backed up for us to ride in style with a glass of champagne to our 'reception'.

The fifty guests all then congregated at Washingborough Hall, run by our goddaughter/niece Lucy (née Fletcher) and her husband Edward Herring. We had Pimms on the lawn, followed by a delicious cold carvery lunch. A magician was employed to work at tables and to entertain the children and celebrations also included our eldest grandson Dan, who had been 21 earlier in the week. Uncle Robert proposed his health and he cut his cake.

Our health was proposed by three sons David, Robert and William and it included a long and funny fax from our eldest, Charles, in Canada. The invitation had been sent out with a vintage wine theme – David built on this and the three boys did a very funny speech about the Bentley grape, a full bodied and well-rounded red and the Margaux grape, originally a young sweet white; softer and less austere than the Bentley, bright and sparkling in appearance!

The family, our 'friends' and particularly Margo and I had a splendid and memorable day.

Lots of looking back and remembering, especially absent friends. A very special toast by our four sons to Mum and Dad/Margo and Bentley and wishes for good health and happiness in the years to come.

A very good time to finish this book, which just possibly should have been titled 'Now Then... and Tomorrow'.

Coleby, July 2013